Talk It Up!

LISTENING, SPEAKING, AND PRONUNCIATION

SECOND EDITION

Joann Rishel Kozyrev

Houghton Mifflin Company   Boston   New York

Editor in Chief: **Patricia A. Coryell**

Director of ESL Publishing: **Susan Maguire**

Senior Development Editor: **Kathy Sands Boehmer**

Editorial Associate: **Manuel Muñoz**

Senior Project Editor: **Kathryn Dinovo**

Manufacturing Manager: **Florence Cadran**

Marketing Manager: **Annamarie Rice**

Marketing Associate: **Claudia Martínez**

Cover image: **Alexander Papaleo**

Photo Credits: **Page xvi** LWA/Dann Tardif/The Stock Market;
page 1 Anton Vengo/SuperStock; page 2 Pictor International/PictureQuest;
page 21 Tom Stewart/The Stock Market; page 24 Bill Aron/PictureQuest;
page 40 Christopher J. De Wolf/Urbanphoto.org;
page 43 Tom Rosenthal/SuperStock; page 63 Bob Wickley/SuperStock;
page 73 IT International/eStock Photography LLC/PictureQuest;
page 82 Jeff Zaruba/The Stock Market; page 85 Bob Wickley/SuperStock;
page 93 David Young-Wolff/PictureQuest; page 103 Jon Feingersh/The Stock Market;
page 121 SuperStock; page 125 Cindy Karp/Black Star Publishing/PictureQuest;
page 134 J. Silver/Superstock; page 145 Tom Rosenthal/Superstock;
page 147 Rim Light/PhotoDisc, Inc.; page 166 David Wolff-Young/Stone

college.hmco.com

Printed in the U.S.A.

Library of Congress Control Number: 2001131518

ISBN: 0-618-14019-0

6789-SB-05

As part of Houghton Mifflin's ongoing
commitment to the environment, this text
has been printed on recycled paper.

Contents

Skills Coverage in **Talk It Up!**   v

Preface   vi

To the Teacher   vi

To the Student   x

Precourse Evaluation   xv

Chapter 1
Friends

Brainstorming   2

Listening One: That's What Friends Are For   3

Listening Two: Excuses, Excuses!   9

Listening Three: Cyberfriends   15

Further Practice   18

Chapter 2
Feeling at Home

Brainstorming: Classified Ads   22

Listening One: A Good Apartment Is Hard to Find   23

Listening Two: Getting Things Fixed   30

Listening Three: What a Neighborhood!   37

Further Practice   40

Chapter 3
Making Connections

Brainstorming: Communication Choices   44

Listening One: E-Mail Connections   45

Listening Two: Send a Card to Stay in Touch   51

Listening Three: Not Another Answering Machine!   57

Further Practice   61

Chapter 4
The World of Work

Brainstorming: Characteristics That Help on the Job   64

Listening One: Getting the Job   65

Listening Two: Breaking the Ice   73

Listening Three: Workplace Challenges   80

Further Practice   82

Chapter 5
School Choices/Life Opportunities

Brainstorming: Help on Campus   86
Listening One: Asking for Advice   87
Listening Two: Learning a Language   93
Listening Three: Being Bilingual—What an Advantage!   100
Further Practice   102

Chapter 6
Money Matters

Brainstorming: Managing Money   104
Listening One: Credit Card or Debit Card? You Decide!   105
Listening Two: Banking by Phone   110
Listening Three: The Trouble with Credit Cards   118
Further Practice   120

Chapter 7
Help!

Brainstorming   126
Listening One: An Emergency!   127
Listening Two: The Missing Wallet   134
Listening Three: Bike Trip Check List   142
Further Practice   143

Chapter 8
Shopping

Brainstorming: Consumer Decisions   146
Listening One: Checking Out   147
Listening Two: Computer Shopping   156
Listening Three: Consumer Watch   164
Further Practice   166

Pairwork Pages

Chapter 3: Practice Pronouncing Contractions   169

Chapter 4: Practice Pronouncing /iy/ and /ɪ/   170

Chapter 5: Practice Pronouncing /s/, /ʃ/, and /tʃ/   170

Chapter 6: Practice Pronouncing /r/ and /l/   171

Chapter 8: Practice Pronouncing /b/, /p/, and /f/   172

Skills Coverage in Talk It Up!

Chapter	Listening Skills	Pronunciation Skills	Speaking Skills	Class Project
1: Friends	Make guesses Support your answers Understand emotions Details Specific information Opinions	Symbols for sounds Syllables	Express an opinion Interview classmates Listen and respond Give and get advice	Advice column
2: Feeling at Home	Specific words Details Main ideas Take notes Attitudes	Syllable stress Schwa	Make and accept invitations Get things fixed	Make a presentation
3: Making Connections	Main ideas Step-by-step order Details Specific information	/ey/, /ɛ/, and /æ/ Contractions	Step-by-step explanations Express sympathy and regret Listen and respond Telephone chain	Create greeting cards
4: The World of Work	Get the gist Implied meaning Main ideas Details Take notes	/iy/ and /ɪ/ Sentence stress	Listen and respond Conduct formal interviews Start a conversation and keep it going	Speak to an expert
5: School Choices/Life Opportunities	Context and attitudes Details Main ideas Take notes	/s/, /ʃ/, and /tʃ/ Intonation	Make suggestions Group discussions	Conduct a survey
6: Money Matters	Predictions Details Follow instructions Specific information Summarize main ideas Take notes	Focal stress /r/ and /l/	Participate in a discussion Call telephone information systems Listen and respond	Work with pie charts
7: Help!	Get the gist Details Supporting information Take notes	/θ/ and /ð/ Linking	Talk with an expert Use toll-free information numbers Listen and respond	Give travel advice
8: Shopping	Understand purpose Listen to numbers Main ideas Details Take notes	Consonant clusters /b/, /p/, and /f/	Compare and contrast Conduct interviews using formal language	Create a radio program

Preface
To the Teacher

About the Program

Talk It Up! is a complete text for the oral communication classroom. It provides activities to help students to build both the fluency and accuracy of their listening and speaking skills. These activities integrate listening, speaking, and pronunciation practice and allow teachers the flexibility to choose the elements of the course that their students need most.

The text is based on the model of oral communication skills shown in the following illustration. Listening, speaking, accuracy (pronunciation), and fluency work together to form the whole that is oral communication. In this model, the listening and speaking skills are represented by two overlapping circles. These skills are inherently related, although they sometimes operate separately.

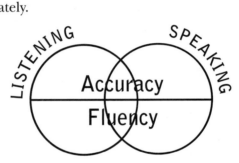

A line through the center of the diagram shows the division between accuracy and fluency.

While these two elements are both parts of the whole, students have the most success when they focus on one of them in a given activity. This is because the focus provides reachable goals, allows students to build specific, useful strategies for improvement, and reduces the frustration that many students feel when faced with the overwhelming task of concentrating simultaneously on meaning, vocabulary, fluency, and accuracy.

The Oral Communication Skills Model

Each chapter in *Talk It Up!* includes various activities from each of the six areas in the oral communication model. Each chapter begins with activities that build fluency in listening, such as listening for main ideas, details, emotion, and meaning in the listening passages. Next, students do pronunciation exercises drawn from the listening passages that they have just heard. These exercises begin with more traditional listening and repeating practice and include production practice. Within each pronunciation section, the production exercises lead from controlled information gap exercises to activities that require more student-generated speech.

After pronunciation practice, students complete spoken fluency activities such as role-playing, chart completion, and guided discussion. At the end of the chapter, activities such as interviews, discussions, guided television viewing, and presentations encourage students to use all of the skills that they have practiced in the chapter. Thus the chapter moves through activities that focus on each of the six areas of the model. This allows students to build all of their oral communication skills, while providing focus and variety for each area of practice. An overview of the chapter sections follows.

Brainstorming

The activities that begin each chapter introduce the topic in an engaging, yet personal way. They also introduce vocabulary and cultural concepts that students will encounter as they work through the chapter. This section focuses largely on the speaking fluency segment of the model.

Listening Activities

The listening activities in the "Talk It Up!" sections correspond to the listening fluency segment of the model. The listening passages also provide the context for the pronunciation and speaking practice that follow each listening section. Each chapter has an overarching theme that focuses on the language that students need as they go about their daily lives, talking with friends, coworkers, and even strangers at work, school, the store, and elsewhere.

The first two listenings in each chapter focus on a variety of functions in the dialogs, including agreeing and disagreeing, requesting assistance, providing encouragement, and extending invitations. The third listening passage is uniquely structured to contain more-challenging, authentic-sounding listening material scripted to sound like the kind of listening that students might hear on answering machines, on the radio, and among friends. The newly revised listening activities in the "Talk It Up!" sections develop a wide variety of global and detail listening skills. These skills are identified in the skills coverage chart that follows the table of contents.

Pronunciation Activities

The pronunciation activities provide practice in each of the three segments of the model that represent accuracy. To ensure a real context for the words and phrases in the pronunciation practice, the examples are taken directly from the language of the listening passages. Each pronunciation section begins with listening practice so that students can practice identifying and repeating the sounds or features. Information exchange and communicative exercises that focus on the target sounds and features help students to bridge the gap between correct production in isolated speech and correct production in longer, less controlled speech segments.

Speaking Activities

Two "Talk It Up!" sections in each chapter provide practice to acquire speaking fluency. The Talk It Up! sections have been revised to more systematically include speaking strategies and language notes that students can use to increase their speaking proficiency. In these sections, students will learn skills such as discussing, interviewing, and telephoning. The progression from listening to speaking and from controlled to more open-ended speech is spiraled through three times in each chapter. This chapter structure facilitates the transfer of the material that students have studied from their controlled English practice into their English communication.

Further Practice

These activities allow students to work on listening and speaking activities at a higher level of complexity. The class projects and other further practice activities encourage students to use their newly developed listening and speaking skills to successfully perform tasks that would have been too difficult prior to their work in the chapter. Also in this section, students are urged to retake the pretests in the preface so that they can chart their own progress in the fluency and accuracy of their speech.

Web Activities

Talk It Up! has a page on the Houghton Mifflin ESL World Wide Web (WWW) site. On this page are activities and links that enable teachers and students to use authentic sources on the Web related to the context and skills taught in each chapter. The activities on the site can be used in classroom, laboratory, or individual study settings.

Sequencing

It is recommended that the preface and the first two chapters be covered in order so that students are exposed to important preliminary pronunciation concepts. The other chapters can be taught in any order to meet the needs of individual programs and classes.

New Features

This edition of *Talk it Up!* includes several improvements:

- streamlined chapter organization
- improved listening activities
- succinct direction lines
- "Talking Points" to highlight language learning strategies
- "On Your Own" activities so that students can continue to learn outside of class
- class projects at the end of each chapter

This edition retains the following elements from the first edition:

- integrated listening, pronunciation, and speaking practice
- useful, interesting topics
- high-quality, engaging listenings
- a variety of speaking skills and strategies
- controlled and communicative pronunciation practice
- self-evaluations for pronunciation and fluency

Preface
To the Student

This preface introduces you to concepts and words that you will use throughout this course. It teaches you about the parts of your mouth and throat that are used to make the sounds of American English, as well as the symbols that this book uses to help you to understand the sounds that you hear. It also teaches you the vocabulary that will help you to talk to your teacher and classmates about pronunciation. It ends with a short speaking test to help you to set goals as you begin the course.

The Speech Organs

To make new sounds in English, you first must learn how to use the speech organs: the lips, teeth, and tongue and other parts of the mouth, as well as the throat. Each time that you study new sounds, you will see a diagram like the following that shows you how to move and use the speech organs to make these sounds. This diagram shows the names of the speech organs that are used to make English sounds.

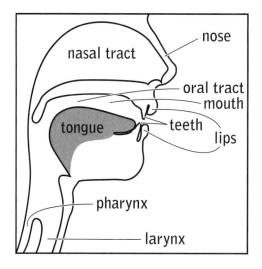

Learning how to position and move the speech organs is the first step toward making sounds correctly. The diagrams are only one tool to help you to do this. Your senses of hearing and touch can also help you to improve your pronunciation. However, the most important way to learn to use the sounds that give you trouble is to practice them every day.

Charts of Sounds and Symbols

The following charts show how the different sounds of American English are made. They also show symbols that represent these sounds. You can use the diagram of the speech organs and the charts of sounds and symbols to help you to understand the way that the sounds are produced. When you are having trouble pronouncing a particular sound, refer to the charts to see how the sounds are made, which speech organs make each sound, and how the organs are positioned to make the sound. However, although the charts are helpful, remember that only through daily practice will you be able to make a sound correctly without thinking about it in your everyday speech.

Consonants

The following chart shows how the consonants in American English are made.

	Two lips	Top teeth & bottom lip	Tongue tip & teeth	Tongue tip & alveolar ridge	Tongue front & hard palate	Tongue in the center	Tongue back & soft palate	Throat
Nasal	m			n			ŋ	
Stop	p b			t d			k g	
Fricative		f v	θ ð	s z	ʃ ʒ			h
Stop & Fricative					tʃ dʒ			
Glides	w			r	y	r	w	
Sides of tongue				l				

The left-hand column tells you where or how the air moves in your mouth or nose.
- *Nasal* means that the air moves out of your nose.
- *Stop* means that you stop and then release the air.
- *Fricative* means that you push the air through a small space between two speech organs, such as your lips, or your tongue and your teeth.
- *Stop and fricative* means that you stop the air and then push it through a small space.
- *Glide* means you move parts of your mouth while making the sound.
- *Sides of tongue* means that you push air around the sides of the tongue.

The top row of the chart shows which vocal organs are used to make each sound. The symbols on the left side of the columns represent *voiceless sounds*—sounds made without vocal chord vibration. The symbols on the right side of the columns represent *voiced sounds*—sounds made with vocal chord vibration. You and your teacher can refer to this chart to help you understand how different American English consonant sounds are made.

Vowels

The following chart shows how the vowels in American English are made. Vowels are more difficult to describe because for many vowel sounds, your tongue does not touch a specific part of your mouth, as it does for consonants. For each vowel sound, you must move your tongue and lips to make your mouth the right shape.

Vowels sounds can be described by whether the tongue is placed high or low in the front, center, or back of the mouth. The following chart shows you the tongue positions for the American English vowel sounds. Note, all vowels are voiced.

- If the symbol for a sound has a /y/ (such as the /iy/ sound in the word *she*), your tongue will move to make a short /y/ sound at the end of the vowel.
- If the symbol for a sound has a /w/ (such as the /ow/ sound in the word *show*), your lips will round at the end of the vowel to make a short /w/ sound.

If you say the sound correctly, it should sound as if the /y/ or /w/ sound follows the vowel sound.

	Front	Central	Back
High	iy		uw
Mid-high	ɪ		ʊ
Mid	ey	ə	ow
Mid-low	ɛ		ɔ
Low	æ		ɑ

Sounds and Rhythm

When thinking about pronunciation, students usually consider only sounds that are difficult for them to hear and say accurately. The English sounds that they find difficult are often the ones not used in their native languages. While these sounds are an important part of pronunciation, the *rhythm* of the language is an even more important part of comprehensible spoken English.

Rhythm is the way that words and sentences are stressed, the intonation used, and the pauses and connections between words. Research shows that non-native rhythm is more likely to be noticed by native speakers of a language than are mispronounced sounds.

It might help you to understand the importance of rhythm to spoken language if you think of language as music. The individual sounds of the language are like the notes of a symphony. Of course it is important for a musician to play the correct notes, but it is more important for the musician to *time* the notes correctly. If the musician plays the notes in the correct order but does not play the correct rhythm, listening to the music is difficult. It also is very important that the musician *not* play notes at certain times. The sign of a master musician is the ability to play all of the right notes with the most expressive rhythm possible. A master musician can do all of this in concert with the other musicians who are performing. The same is true of a communicator. This book is designed to help you to become a master communicator using the English language as your instrument.

Strategies for Improving Pronunciation

Learning how to pronounce English correctly takes time and practice, but you can do some things to help your pronunciation improve more quickly. Good pronunciation consists of many skills. By focusing your attention on the skill that you need, you will gradually improve. In some ways, improving your pronunciation is like learning to play a new sport.

- **Listen: Practice hearing difficult sounds correctly.**

Learning to hear new sounds and rhythms is like collecting the equipment that you need to play a sport. You cannot play volleyball until you have at least a net and a ball.

- **Physical practice: Train yourself to use the parts of your mouth, nasal passages, and throat to make the sounds of English.**

When you play a sport, you use the muscles in your body to play well. You have to know how to move your muscles, and you have to practice to make them stronger.

- **Speak naturally: Practice daily so that you learn to pronounce the sounds and rhythm of English automatically and naturally.**

Sports have rules, and you must be sure that you follow those rules when you play. You have to think about the rules when you play, but the more that you play the game correctly, the more naturally you can play without consciously thinking about the rules.

- **Get help: Consult your teacher and classmates as if they were your coach and teammates.**

When you play a sport, you can get help in many ways. You can work with a coach, who will teach you the sport, and you can learn from your teammates, who will help you to play better. However, you will become a good athlete only if you spend a lot of time playing, exercising, and practicing.

Precourse Evaluation

Some students find it difficult to practice speaking and listening effectively because it is hard for them to decide how to focus on improving. You might think that you must focus on pronunciation, vocabulary, fluency, grammar, and meaning all at the same time—and with no time to go back and fix mistakes! However, you can focus on different areas of your listening and speaking if you know which areas are important for you to improve. The following two tests will help you and your teacher to choose the areas of oral communication on which you should focus. Every two chapters, you will have the opportunity to evaluate yourself again to see if you are meeting your goals and to help you to set new goals. Each time that you take the test, you or your teacher should record your progress in the chart on page xviii. This chart will show your progress throughout the course. Keep in mind that progress in any area requires practice and that you and your teacher should focus on the areas that are most important to your improving the comprehensibility of your speech.

Fluency Pretest

The following test will help you to see how fluently and easily you can speak about a familiar topic.

1. Study the picture on the next page for one minute. Do not use a dictionary or take notes about the things in the picture.

2. Record a description of the picture on tape. Talk for about one minute. Try to speak as fluently as you can. Make your pauses as natural as possible.

3. Listen to the tape, and give yourself a score using the following scoring system. Write your score in the Self-Evaluation Record-Keeping Chart on page xviii in the space for Fluency Pretest.

4—Very fluent: The pauses are natural, and the speech is very easy to understand. There is little problem with word choice.
3—Fluent: There are some unnatural pauses, and occasionally you cannot think of a word, but the meaning is still clear.
2—Somewhat fluent: Sometimes your meaning is difficult to understand because of many unnatural pauses. You have some trouble thinking of the right word.
1—Not fluent: Usually your meaning is difficult to understand because of unnatural pauses or because you have problems thinking of the right word.

Pronunciation Pretest

As you begin to use this book, think about the pronunciation problems on which you want to work. You will make the most progress if you select only one or two features of your speech and then focus on them until you are pleased with the results. Then you can choose a new focus.

To help you to choose your pronunciation focus, record yourself reading the following passage. Then listen to the recorded passage with your teacher. Listen for the sounds and features of your speech that seem to make your speech difficult to understand. Look at the charts earlier in this preface to help you to identify the problem sounds. Improving these sounds and features should be your first goal. Write these problem features and sounds in the Self-Evaluation Record-Keeping Chart in the space for Pronunciation Pretest.

Staying in Touch

What is your favorite way to stay in touch with family and friends? One of the cheapest is the old-fashioned letter. When you write a letter, you can think carefully about what you want to say and write all about what you're doing and how you feel.

Telephone calls are much faster than letters. People usually like to call a friend or family member so that they can hear each other's voices, but telephone calls can be expensive. Is calling too expensive? Do you dislike writing letters? Well, here's a good way to communicate naturally for a reasonable cost. All you need is a tape recorder and a tape. You can record everything that you want to say and send it to your friends or family. You can even record some of your favorite music, your dog barking, or other sounds to make the tape interesting. If they want, your friends and family can record a message on the other side of the tape and send the tape back to you.

Now that you have completed the test, look at the score and comments that you made in the chart for Pronunciation Pretest. Decide what areas of your speech need the most improvement. These areas will be your focus for the first part of the course. Consult your teacher if you need help choosing your focus. Write the focus (or foci) that you choose in the chart.

Self-Evaluation Record-Keeping Chart

Fluency Test No.	Score	Comments
Pretest		
1		
2		
3		
4		
Pronunciation Test No.	Problems with Sounds, Stress, or Intonation	Comments
Pretest		
1		
2		
3		
4		

Acknowledgments

Many teachers and students have contributed to the development of *Talk It Up!*. I am especially grateful to the editorial team at Houghton Mifflin: Susan Maguire for her vision and support; Kathy Sands Boehmer for her gentle, inspiring guidance; and Manuel Muñoz for his steady support and insight. I am especially pleased with the design and layout created by Cindy Johnson of Publishing Services, and I'm thankful for the extra effort she and her team put into finding photographs for the book. I also wish to thank my colleagues for their feedback and suggestions, especially Marni Baker Stein, whose contributions to the series encouraged and uplifted me. I am indebted to the teachers and students who have used the first edition of this book and given me invaluable feedback. The following reviewers provided their expertise and many useful suggestions:

Joyce Hutchings, Georgetown University

Janine Rudnick, El Paso Community College

Richard Sansone, Valencia Community College

Hollis M. Shaw, Houston Community College, North

1

Friends

CHAPTER HIGHLIGHTS

Listening	Pronunciation	Speaking	Class Project
Make guesses	Symbols for sounds	Interview classmates	Create an advice column
Support your answers	Syllables	Listen and respond	
Understand emotions		Express an opinion	
Listen for details		Give and get advice	
Listen for specific information			
Understand opinions			

Brainstorming

English has several words that describe friends. Match the following words to their descriptions.

a. friend

b. close or best friend

c. acquaintance

d. colleague

e. boyfriend or girlfriend

1. __d__ a person with whom you work

2. __e__ a romantic friend

3. __b__ a person whom you can trust very much; someone who shares important parts of your life

4. __a__ a person whom you know and like being with

5. __c__ a person whom you know but not very well

How many words describe friends in your native language? Explain what each of these words means as accurately as you can.

Listening One
That's What Friends Are For

Kim and Viki are friends at college. They are sitting in the student union talking about their plans for the weekend.

Before You Listen

What do you expect from your friends? Make sure that you understand all of the following phrases. Then mark three of them that express what you think close friends should do.

____ spend time together

____ influence each other

____ have fun together

____ get along with each other

____ be inseparable

____ help each other

____ make new friends together

____ share the same sense of humor

Compare your choices with those of others in your class. Explain why you made these choices.

Listen to Make Guesses

 Read the following statements, and then listen to Kim and Viki's conversation. Based on what you hear, guess whether each statement is true or false and circle the correct answer.

1. Kim is excited that her friend Gwen is coming to visit.   True   False

2. Gwen is shy.   True   False

3. Now it is easy for Kim to make friends.   True   False

Listen to Support Your Answers

Listen again to Kim and Viki's conversation. In the following list, mark the statement from the conversation that supports your answers in the previous exercise.

1. _____ I really miss her.

   _____ You guys were close in school?

   _____ I really changed because of her.

2. _____ She's got a great sense of humor.

   _____ I was really nervous about meeting people.

   _____ She showed me how to talk to people.

3. _____ How would you describe me? Shy?

   _____ It's not that easy if you don't know how.

   _____ I want to have a party for her with all my friends here.

Compare your answers with those of a small group of your classmates, and explain why you think that your answers are correct.

After You Listen

Read the following proverbs about friends. Find out what each proverb means. Do you agree with each one? Why or why not?

1. Make new friends, but keep the old. One is silver, and the other is gold.

2. A friend in need is a friend indeed.

3. It's good to have friends in high places.

Does your native language have similar proverbs? If yes, explain them to your classmates.

Pronunciation ACTIVITIES

Symbols for Sounds

You already know the twenty-six letters of the alphabet that are used to spell words in English. You probably also know that one letter can represent many different sounds. This is because American English has about thirty-nine sounds. There simply aren't enough letters to represent all of the sounds.

Because there are more sounds than letters, a system is needed for writing sounds so that there is less confusion about which sound is being shown. This book uses an adaptation of the Smith-Trager system to represent the sounds of American English.

Voiced Consonants		Voiceless Consonants		Vowels (Voiced)	
/b/	**b**ig	/p/	**p**en	/iy/	s**ee**n
/m/	**m**an			/ɪ/	d**i**d
/w/	**w**oman			/ey/	pl**ay**
/v/	**v**owel	/f/	**f**ight	/ɛ/	s**e**nd
/n/	**n**ice			/æ/	b**a**d
/d/	**d**one	/t/	**t**op	/ə/	**a**bout
/z/	**z**ero	/s/	**s**ing	/a/	j**o**b
/l/	**l**ight			/uw/	bl**ue**
/r/	**r**ed			/ʊ/	sh**ou**ld
/ð/	**th**at	/θ/	**th**ing	/ow/	kn**ow**
/ʒ/	u**s**ual	/ʃ/	**sh**op	/ɔ/	br**ough**t
/dʒ/	**j**ob	/tʃ/	**ch**ange	/ay/	fl**y**
/y/	**y**ear			/aw/	br**ow**n
/g/	**g**et	/k/	**k**ind	/ɔy/	c**oi**n
/ŋ/	bri**ng**				
		/h/	**h**elp		

Notice that consonants are listed in two groups. The first group is called *voiced consonants,* and the second is called *voiceless consonants.* Some sounds are made by vibrating the vocal cords. These sounds are called *voiced sounds.* You can feel your vocal cords vibrate when you make these sounds if you put your hand on your throat while you speak. All vowels and the consonants in the left column are voiced sounds.

Some sounds are made without any vibration of the vocal cords. These are called *voiceless sounds.* If you put your hand on your throat while you say a voiceless sound, you will not feel any movement. The consonants in the middle column are all voiceless sounds. Notice that in this chart sounds that are made the same way except for a difference in voicing are placed next to each other.

The following exercises will help you to learn the symbols that this book uses to represent the sounds of English.

The following words are written using the symbols in the previous chart. Read each word, and then write its regular English spelling on the line.

1. wiykɛnd   _weekend_
2. əbawt   _about_
3. klows   _close_
4. aydiyə   _idea_
5. tʃeyndʒd   _changed_
6. bəfɔr   _before_
7. ɪkstriymliy   _extramely_
8. kanvərseyʃən   _conversation_
9. iyziy   _easy_
10. təgɛðɛr   _togher_

For more practice with sounds and symbols, work with a partner. Choose one word from each of the following groups. Pronounce the word. Your partner should be able to point to the word that you said. After you have read one word from each group, switch roles with your partner.

1. partiy	pæst	piypəl
2. want	wət	wʊd
3. gowɪŋ	gɛtɪŋ	grɛyt
4. awər	haw	hiyr
5. mɛt	meyd	mæθ
6. miyn	mɪs	mɪyt
7. wiyk	wɛrk	wɛr
8. ʃay	ʃiy	siyn
9. lats	layk	layks
10. kiypɪŋ	kalɪŋ	keym

TALK
It Up!

Interviewing Classmates

Interviewing Skills

A great way to practice your speaking, pronunciation, and listening skills is to interview classmates and other people. Whenever you interview someone, you should follow these steps.

1. Plan the interview. Decide whom you will interview and what questions you will ask.

2. Introduce yourself to the person whom you want to interview. Explain the subject of the interview and why you are doing the interview.

3. Ask the person's permission to ask him or her the questions.

   Example: "Excuse me. My name is Manuel Ricardo. I'm interviewing people about friendship for my English assignment. Would you mind if I asked you a few questions?"

   Example: "Hello. I'm Lisa, and I'm doing an interview for my English class. Could I ask you three questions about friendship?"

4. Do not take too much of the person's time. Also, do not try to write down every word that the person says. Instead, take notes or record the interview, and then fill in the details after you have finished the interview. Ask only as many questions as you need to get all of the necessary information. Three to five questions are usually enough.

5. When you have finished asking the questions, thank the person for his or her time.

   Use these interviewing techniques whenever you do interviews in this and the following chapters.

Practice Interviewing Skills

To practice these interviewing skills, interview some of your classmates about their closest friends. Ask questions about how your classmates met their friends and how those friends have influenced them.

1. Plan the interview by deciding what questions you will ask. Read the following information about question types and typical responses, and then do the activities that follow.

Question Types and Typical Responses

In an interview, different types of questions get different types of answers. Some questions encourage short answers, and others encourage longer answers. Look at the following types of questions and the answers that will probably result from them.

Yes/No question: This type of question gets the shortest answers. People usually respond only with the word *yes* or *no*.

> **Example:** "Do you ask your friends for advice?"
> "Yeah, sometimes."

Who, What, When, or Where question: This type of question usually gets a short answer that is only a few words long.

> **Example:** "Who are your closest friends?"
> "Andy and Beth, I guess."

> **Example:** "When do you spend time with your friends?"
> "I usually see them on the weekends."

How or Why question: This type of question requires a longer answer, usually one or more sentences. This kind of question is most likely to get a conversation going.

> **Example:** "Why is it important to have close friends?"
> "Good friends help you to feel good about yourself. And they can really help you out when you have problems."

2. Brainstorm a list of four or five questions that you could ask the people whom you interview. Write below at least one question of each type you have read about in this chapter. Discuss the questions and the types of answers that you would expect to hear if you asked them.

Example: *Who is your closest friend, and how did you meet?*

_____

_____

_____

_____

_____

3. On your own, choose three questions from the list that you want
    to ask. Write the questions that you chose in the following
    Interviewing Chart.

Interviewing Chart

Questions	Name	Name	Name

4. Interview each classmate in your group. Before beginning an inter-
    view, write in the chart the name of the classmate. Then note in the
    chart the answers that the classmate gives you. Do not write every
    word of the answer. Simply make notes that will help you to remember
    the answer.

5. In a new group of classmates, summarize the information in your chart
    for the members of the new group.

Listening Two
Excuses, Excuses!

Ken is supposed to meet Viki at 7:00 P.M. to go to Kim's party. It's 8:05 P.M.,
and Viki's telephone rings.

Before You Listen

**Write your answers to the following questions. Then, explain to other class-
mates the reasons for your answers.**

1. When you meet someone, are you usually
    a. late?
    b. early?
    c. on time?

2. How long will you wait for someone who is late?

    a.   fifteen minutes

    b.   less than an hour

    c.   over an hour

3. How do you feel when a friend is late?

    a.   angry

    b.   worried

    c.   impatient

Listen to Understand Emotions

 Listen to the conversation, and answer the following questions.

1. How does Viki feel?   2. How does Ken feel?

    a.   bored   a.   impatient

    b.   tired   b.   worried

    c.   angry   c.   apologetic

Listen for Detail

 Listen to the conservation again to hear the answers to the following questions. Mark all of the correct answers with an X.

1. Viki thinks Ken is late because

    _____ he doesn't care about their friendship.

    _____ he has had an accident.

    _____ he doesn't want to go to the party.

2. Ken says he is late because

    _____ he didn't think about the time.

    _____ he likes his other friends better than Viki.

    _____ he thought Viki didn't care when they left.

3. When Viki says "How nice of you to call!" she really means:

    _____ "I'm glad you called me."

    _____ "You should have called sooner."

    _____ "Don't ever call me again."

Listen and Respond

 Listen to the beginning of this conversation. When the recording stops, finish the conversation with a partner. Your conversation might end differently than Ken and Viki's or in the same way. Be prepared to share your ending with the class.

TALKING POINT

Imitating recorded (or real-life) conversations can help you to be prepared if you must speak spontaneously in a similar situation. This learning strategy is called "rehearsing."

After You Listen

Discuss the following questions with a small group of your classmates. Share your answers with others in the class.

1. What do you do when you are angry with someone? Do you talk to him or her about the problem, or do you decide not to talk about it?

2. What do you do when someone does not apologize and you think that he or she should?

Pronunciation ACTIVITIES

Syllables

Every English word has one or more syllables. A *syllable* is a part of a word. The sounds in a syllable are said together with no interruptions, almost as if they are said as one sound. In English, a syllable has one vowel sound and might have several consonant sounds.

Some words, such as these, have only one syllable:
one, where, you, thought

Others have two syllables, such as these:
wait-ing, friend-ship, wor-ry

And others have three or more syllables:
ac-ci-dent, im-pa-tient

Practice Hearing Syllables

Listen for the following words from the conversation between Ken and Viki, and write the number of syllables that you hear.

1. _____ waiting
2. _____ over
3. _____ already
4. _____ guess
5. _____ important

6. _____ called
7. _____ accident
8. _____ anyway
9. _____ right
10. _____ sorry

TALKING POINT

If you are having difficulty hearing syllables, listen again and use your pencil or finger to tap the book for each syllable that you hear.

More Practice with Syllables

Poetry such as limericks and haiku require a specific number of syllables in each line. Count the syllables in these two poems to learn the syllable rules.

Limerick

Number of syllables per line

_____ I've a friend who's in all my classes,

_____ Who wants all his grades to be passes.

_____ So he studies hard all night

_____ Without a strong enough light.

_____ Soon I think we'll see him in glasses.

Haiku

Number of syllables per line

_____ Never be a frog

_____ Who opens his mouth so wide

_____ He shows all inside.

Kago no Chiyo (1703–1775)

Practice reading these poems out loud, pronouncing the correct number of syllables in each line.

TALK It Up!

Expressing an Opinion Politely

Sometimes you need to express an opinion that differs from someone else's. Many ways are available to phrase an opinion politely in English.

- Use the words "I think" to let others know that this is your opinion.
- State the reasons for your opinion.
- Use words such as *might, could, would,* and *if.* These words are rather indirect.

Remember that many situations are possible in which it is important that you state your opinion directly.

- It is not impolite to disagree very directly if you are being asked to do something that you believe is morally wrong or dangerous.
- It is acceptable to state your opinion directly, but politely, if someone is not fulfilling his or her responsibilities at work or school.
- In some close friendships, it is acceptable to disagree directly; this depends on the individual relationship.

Disagreeing Directly and Indirectly

Disagreeing with someone is not as easy as agreeing with someone. When you disagree with a friend, it is not always easy to tell your friend what you think without hurting his or her feelings. Sometimes it is alright to say directly what you think, and sometimes you need to be indirect in expressing your feelings.

For example, suppose that your friend gets a new haircut that you do not like and asks you, "What do you really think? Do you like it?" You could indirectly say, "It's nice, but I thought that your hair looked really nice the old way." However, if your friend shows you a picture of a haircut that he or she is thinking about getting and asks your opinion, you might decide to be more direct and say, "No, I don't like that style. Are you sure that's what you want?"

Phrases for Agreeing and Disagreeing

1   2   3

Very indirect   Very direct

For each of the following phrases, write the number from this scale that shows how direct or indirect each phrase sounds to you.

1. ـــــ That's a really silly idea.
2. ـــــ I wouldn't do that if I were you.
3. ـــــ Have you thought about any other ways to solve this problem?
4. ـــــ You're wrong. That's not what happened.
5. ـــــ To tell you the truth, I wanted to do it a different way.
6. ـــــ Are you sure that's right?
7. ـــــ I thought that you said you were going to do it Friday.
8. ـــــ You told me that you would do it Friday.
9. ـــــ I have to say, I think that there could be a better answer.
10. ـــــ What were you thinking? That will never work!

In a group of your classmates, compare your answers and explain why you gave each statement the ranking that you did. Summarize your group's discussion for a new group or for the class.

Read the following situations. For each, choose a phrase from the previous list, or think of a phrase of your own that you might use to disagree with the person. Discuss your choices with others in your class.

1. A fellow student did not come to a meeting that was scheduled in order to work on a group project. She says no one told her about the meeting, but you heard another student tell her. What would you say if
   a.   this is the first meeting that your classmate has missed?
   b.   this is the third meeting that your classmate has missed?

2. Your friend has planned a trip for the two of you. He has planned to go to a place that he should know you do not want to visit. How would you tell him that you do not want to go there if
   a.   he is your closest friend?
   b.   he is not a very close friend?

3. A friend who has been car shopping tells you about a car. The car sounds like a bad deal to you. What would you say to your friend if
   a.   your friend asks for your advice about the car before buying it?
   b.   your friend has already bought the car?
   c.   your friend plans to buy the car, but does not ask for your advice?

Practice Agreeing and Disagreeing

Imagine that you are having a discussion with the people who made the following statements. List the ways in which you could respond to each. Do not say simply, "I agree" or "I disagree"; rather, give a reason for your opinion. Refer back to the box on disagreeing before you begin.

1. I think that you have to meet your closest friends when you are a child. People who are friends from childhood are always closer than people who became friends as adults.

2. The best way to meet people is to walk up to someone and start talking.

3. The best friends are people who are a lot like you. As the saying goes, "Birds of a feather flock together."[1] That is, you should be friends with people with whom you have a lot in common.

Listening Three
Cyberfriends

Before You Listen

You will hear some students talking about how the Internet can be used to meet new people. You might not understand every word that the students say the first time that you listen. That is all right. Focus on what you do understand. You will have opportunities to discuss the information and to listen again.

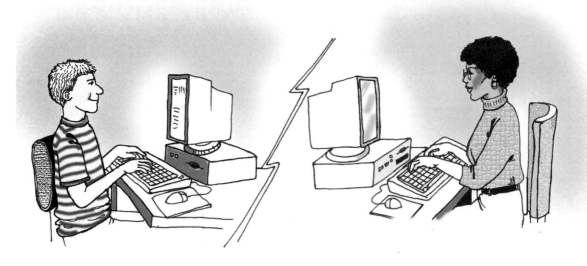

[1]This saying means that people who have similar interests will be friends just as birds that are similar stay together.

Think about the following questions, and write your answers in note form. Then compare your answers with a partner or in a small group.

1. Would you agree to meet a person whom you have never met if your friend knew the person and wanted to introduce you? Why or why not?

   _____

2. Would you agree to meet someone from whom you had received letters or computer messages if you had never talked to that person? Why or why not?

   _____

3. Can people who have never met in person become friends? If you know of people who have met only through letters or e-mail and become friends, share their stories with the class.

   _____

Share the results of your discussion with your class, or record your answers to the questions on tape for homework.

Listen for Specific Information

 Listen to hear whether the students say that they have used the Internet. Write the answers in the first row of the chart.

Question	First Student	Second Student	Third Student
Does this person say he or she uses the Internet?			
What does this person think of using the Internet to make friends?			

Listen to Hear Opinions

Listen again to hear each speaker's opinion about meeting people on the Internet. Note the answers in the second row of the chart.

Listen to Language

Listen to each speaker's opinion again. This time, pay special attention to the way that the speakers agree and disagree with each other. Write the phrases that they use on these lines, and then answer the questions that follow.

_____

_____

1. Do these students disagree with one another directly or indirectly?

2. How well do you believe that these students know each other? Why do you think so?

3. How do the students phrase their opinions so that they do not say anything impolite?

After You Listen

With a small group of your classmates, use the notes that you took in the previous chart to identify the good points and bad points of making friends on the Internet. Your group should add at least three of its own ideas to each column. You do not have to agree with an idea in order to write it down.

Good Points of Internet Friendships   Bad Points of Internet Friendships

_____   _____

_____   _____

_____   _____

_____   _____

_____   _____

_____   _____

_____   _____

Further Practice

Watching Television

Many television comedy shows concern a problem between friends or family members. Often the problem is solved in the half hour or hour that the show airs on television. Although solving all problems so quickly is not very realistic, you can learn a lot of language regarding disagreements by watching these shows.

Watch any television comedy show, and fill in the following questionnaire. Report on the show you watched to a group of classmates.

Name of the show: _____

Channel: _____

Which characters have a problem during the show? _____

_____

What is the problem? _____

_____

How is it solved? _____

_____

What words and phrases did you learn from the show? _____

_____

Giving and Getting Advice

Sometimes very good friends get into arguments that they really want to resolve, but they do not know how. When this happens, they will sometimes ask someone else for advice.

Read about the following three problems. With a group of your classmates, choose one or more of the problems and discuss the advice that you would give this person. Try to agree on how to solve the problem.

1. My friend is always late meeting me. I don't mean that she comes five or ten minutes late. She's always at least thirty minutes late, and it's not unusual for her to come an hour after the time that we agreed on. She knows it's a problem; she just always tries to do more in a day than she can. But I'm tired of waiting for her. What should I do?

2. I told a coworker of mine about a problem that I'm having at work. It wasn't a big deal. I just told her about a disagreement that I had with our boss. I didn't want her to tell others at work, but she did. Now I'm afraid that the boss will find out that I complained. I'm really mad at her. She says she was only trying to help! What should I do?

3. A friend is living with me for a year while he is in college. He's always watching TV or listening to the stereo. Sometimes he turns on the TV with no sound and watches it and at the same time listens to his CDs and tapes on the stereo. I ask him to turn down the audio, and he always does, but this situation is starting to drive me crazy! I feel like I am being too picky, since he likes his music, but I would like at least an hour of quiet every now and then. Other than this problem, he's a great person to live with. What should I do?

Class Project: Create an Advice Column

Many newspapers have an advice column in which you can read a letter from someone who has a problem. Then the person who writes the column answers the letter in the newspaper, giving the letter writer some advice.

Find in your local newspaper an advice column, and take it to class. With a group of your classmates, choose a letter from one of the columns and then answer the following questions about it.

1. What problem does the letter writer have?

2. What advice does the column writer give?

3. Do you and your classmates agree with the advice? Why or why not?

4. What different advice would you and your classmates give?

As a class, start an advice column by following these steps.

1. Put a box in the classroom in which students can put letters that describe real or imaginary problems that they are having. The letters should be confidential, so the writer should use a false name.

2. Meet in small groups to decide on advice to give to the letter writers.

3. Publish a newsletter with advice about the problems, or post the letters and answers on a bulletin board at school.

2

Feeling
at Home

Listening	Pronunciation	Speaking	Class Project
Listen for specific words	Syllable stress	Make and accept invitations	Give an oral presentation
Listen for main ideas	Schwa	Get things fixed	
Listen for details			
Understand attitudes			
Take notes			

Brainstorming

Classified Ads

Look at the classified ads that follow or at similar ads in a local newspaper. Find an apartment for each person in the following descriptions. Write the telephone number that each person should call to find out more about the apartment that you chose for him or her.

APARTMENTS FOR RENT

Nice 2BR, furnished, new kitchen and paint, quiet building, pkg., affordable rent, 555-1220

GARDEN APARTMENTS
678 N Broad Street
2 and 3 BR

- kitchen with all appliances
- convenient location
- swimming pool
- 24 hr. maintenance service
- low deposit
- reasonable rates

555-6756

BEAUTIFUL! 1BR and 2BR townhouses, modern kitchen, W/D, AC, pets and families welcome. CALL 555-7491

Deluxe 1BR apt. w/ all appliances, carpet, clean, on busline, deposit and lease req. 555-4310

Efficiency, 365 E. Summit Dr., furnished, great for students, $500/mo, 555-1295

Best of Everything!
New Spacious 2BR apartments, with balcony, nicely decorated, close to campus, available immediately—call for application.
555-0909

Classified ad vocabulary

AC = air conditioning

appliances = electrical machines for household use, such as a refrigerator

BR = bedroom

efficiency = a one room apartment with a small kitchen and bathroom

lease = a written agreement between the landlord and the renter

pkg. = parking

req. = required

townhouse = houses in a row and having two floors

W/D= washer and dryer

Descriptions

1. Chad is a student. He does not want to live in a residence hall, but he cannot afford a large apartment. He wants to live near his college so that he can walk to school. _____

2. Rick works at night. He needs an apartment where he will have quiet neighbors because he sleeps in the daytime. _____

3. Lupe has a job in town and must always be on time for work. She has a car, but it is old and breaks down a lot. She needs an apartment and will live with a roommate if necessary. _____

4. Wendy and Lamar will have their first baby in six months. They also have a dog. They live in a one-bedroom apartment now, but they want something larger. _____

Compare your answers in a small group of classmates or with your entire class. Explain why you think that the apartment you chose would be good for each person.

Listening One
A Good Apartment Is Hard to Find

Dave sees Barbara in the college bookstore. He invites her to a house-warming party that he and his wife Jill are having at their new apartment. And she talks about the kind of apartment that she would like to rent.

Before You Listen

Read this party invitation, and then answer the questions that follow.

1. Dave and Jill have moved to a new home.   True   False
2. Dave and Jill are moving on Friday.   True   False
3. Guests are expected to bring food to the party.   True   False
4. Guests should call to tell Dave and Jill whether they
   can come.   True   False

Listen for Specific Words

Listen to the conversation, and mark in the following list each kind of home that Dave and Barbara discuss.

_____ apartment

_____ townhouse

_____ dormitory

_____ house

_____ one-room apartment

_____ cottage

Listen for Details

Listen again, and then answer the following questions.

1. When is Dave and Jill's party?
    a. tonight at 7:00 P.M.
    b. tonight at 7:30 P.M.
    c. tomorrow at 7:00 P.M.
    d. tomorrow at 7:30 P.M.

2. Why does Barbara want to leave the dorm?

    a.   so that she can concentrate on her studies better

    b.   because the dorms are too expensive

    c.   so that she can have a roommate

    d.   because she does not want to buy a car

3. What problem does Barbara have with apartments close to campus?

    a.   She can't concentrate because there is too much noise.

    b.   They are very expensive.

    c.   She would have to pay a lot for transportation.

    d.   They do not have both a bedroom and a living room.

4. What problem does Barbara have with apartments out of town?

    a.   She cannot concentrate there because there is too much noise.

    b.   They are very expensive.

    c.   She would have to pay a lot for transportation.

    d.   They do not have both a bedroom and a living room.

5. What kind of apartment will Barbara probably rent?

    a.   an apartment at Garden Apartments

    b.   an apartment close to campus

    c.   an apartment out of town

    d.   a one-room apartment

After You Listen: Accepting an Invitation

Imagine that you have been invited to Dave and Jill's housewarming party. With a partner, role-play a telephone conversation between Dave (or Jill) and a guest who is calling to say that he or she will come to the house-warming party. Be prepared to present your role-play to others in your class.

Pronunciation ACTIVITIES

Syllable Stress

In English, one syllable in each word is stressed more than the other syllables. A stressed syllable has a longer, louder, and higher sound than the other syllables in the word. The following picture shows how the syllable stress in the word "invited" would look if you could see it. The stressed syllable is the high point in the picture.

Here are three rules to help you to predict syllable stress.

In-VIT-ed

Rule No. 1: When a two-syllable word can be both a verb and a noun or adjective, the verb form is usually stressed on the second syllable and the noun or adjective form is usually stressed on the first syllable.

Examples:

PREsent	(adjective)	Everyone in our class is present today.
PREsent	(noun)	She gave her friend a lovely present.
preSENT	(verb)	The students presented their teacher with a birthday card.

Rule No. 2: Prefixes and suffixes are usually not stressed.

Examples:

walk + -ing	=	WALKing
un- + clear	=	unCLEAR
thought + -ful	=	THOUGHTful
help + less	=	HELPless
im + possible	=	imPOSSible

Rule No. 3: Words with some suffixes are usually stressed on the syllable just *before* the suffix. These suffixes include

-tion   -cian   -sion   -ic   -ity   -ical   -ify   -ogy   -graphy

Examples:

-tion	-cian	-sion
exAM examinAtion	TECHnical techNIcian	disCUSS disCUSSion

-ic	-ity	-ify
eLECtric	elecTRICity	eLECtrify

-ical	-ogy	-graphy
geoLOGical	geOLogy	geOgraphy

Practice Syllable Stress in Words

In each of the following words, underline the syllable that you predict will be stressed. Then, listen to each word and check your predictions.

Example: <u>Bar</u>bara

1. tomorrow
2. apartment
3. rented
4. concentrate
5. expensive
6. concentration
7. looking
8. classified
9. transportation
10. spend

Listen to the words again and repeat after the speaker. Be sure to stress the correct syllable.

Practice Syllable Stress in Sentences

In the following sentences from the conversation, underline each word that has more than one syllable. Then, for each underlined word, circle the syllable that should be stressed. Listen to check your predictions.

1. Jill and I want to invite you to our house-warming party.
2. I need a place where I can concentrate when I study.
3. That won't help my concentration.
4. Everything close to campus is really expensive.
5. You could look for a one-room apartment.

Communicative Pronunciation Practice

Add three questions to the following list. Mark the syllable stress in all words that have more than one syllable. The first is done for you. Practice pronouncing the syllable stress by answering the question with others in your class or on tape.

1. What three <u>qualities</u> should the <u>perfect</u> <u>room</u>mate have?
2. Name one household appliance that you can't live without. Why?

3. What is the most interesting invitation you have ever received?

4. _____

5. _____

6. _____

Just for Fun

Do English speakers often mispronounce your name? Do they use the same number of syllables or stress one syllable more than others?

Draw a picture of the way that English speakers say your name. Then draw a picture that shows the way that you say your name in your language. Show both pictures to your class. Explain why people make the mistakes that they do.

TALK It Up!

Invitations

Inviting people to visit your home or to do something together is a great way to get to know them and to practice your English. Dave invites Barbara to his party by saying, "Jill and I want to invite you to our housewarming party tomorrow night. It's potluck. 7:00. Apartment 30B." This is a good invitation because it answers the following questions.

- Who is making the invitation?
- What kind of event is planned?
- When is the event (day and time)?
- Where is the event?

An invitation does not always answer all of these questions in the first sentence. Sometimes the last two questions are answered after the invitee has accepted the invitation.

Here are some other phrases that you can use to make invitations to

- **a party at your house:** "My friends and I are planning an international dinner party at my house. Would you like to come?"
- **a lunch for which you plan to pay:** "I'd like to take you out for lunch—my treat!"
- **a lunch at which you plan to split the bill with your friend:** "I'm getting kind of hungry. Would you like to go somewhere for lunch?"
- **a study session:** "Maybe we could study for the test together? We could meet in the library on Thursday."

With a partner, choose one of the situations in the previous box. On the following lines, write a short dialog in which one partner makes an invitation and the other accepts the invitation. Use either the suggested phrase or different words.

A: _____

B: _____

A: _____

B: _____

A: _____

B: _____

Present your dialog to others in your class. Decide which invitations are

1. the most formal:

   _____

2. the most inviting:

   _____

3. the simplest:

   _____

4. the most direct:

   _____

Listening Two
Getting Things Fixed

Yesterday, Jill called the maintenance office because her stove is broken. She and Dave are having their house-warming party tonight, and they need to cook. She calls the repair office again, because no one has come to fix the stove yet.

Before You Listen

If you rent an apartment, what do you do when something in your apartment does not work? Read each of the possible following actions, and mark the appropriate ones.

____ Call the landlord's office or maintenance office, and ask to have it fixed.

____ Call a repair service, and send the bill to the landlord.

____ Try to fix it yourself so that you do not bother the landlord.

____ Stop paying your rent until the problem is fixed.

Compare your suggestions with a partner. Decide which you agree on or like the best.

Listen for the Main Idea

 Listen to Jill's telephone call, and choose the best answer to the following question: Is the problem solved?

____ Jill knows that the problem is solved.

____ Jill thinks that the problem is solved.

____ The problem cannot be solved.

____ The problem will be solved tomorrow.

Listen for Details

Listen to the dialog again. Answer the following questions.

1. Jill lives in apartment
   a.   30B.
   b.   30P.
   c.   13B.
   d.   13P.

2. The man who does appliance repairs
   a. came yesterday.
   b. has not come.
   c. came but did not fix the stove.
   d. cannot come today.

3. Jill asks the worker at the maintenance office to
   a. apologize because she has had to wait.
   b. come to her house and look at the stove.
   c. tell her the name of the worker who fixes appliances.
   d. call her back and tell her when the worker will come.

Take Notes: Telephone Messages

 You work at the maintenance office, and you just got Jill's telephone call. Use the following message form to note all of the information that Mr. Whitman needs in order to fix Jill's stove right away.

While you were out...

For: _____

Time: _____ Date: _____

Mr./Ms. _____

of _____

Phone _____

Telephoned		Please call	
Was in to see you		Will call again	
Wants to see you		Returned your call	
URGENT			

Message _____

_____

_____

_____

Message taken by _____

After You Listen

Use your notes to role-play the following conversations with a partner.

1. The worker in the maintenance office calls Mr. Whitman to give him Jill's message.

2. The worker in the maintenance office calls Jill to tell her when Mr. Whitman will arrive.

Pronunciation
ACTIVITIES

The /ə/ Sound in Unstressed Syllables

You know that stressed syllables have longer, louder, and higher sounds than do unstressed syllables. When native speakers of English pronounce the sounds in unstressed syllables quickly and quietly, the vowel sound in these syllables often changes to the sound /ə/. This sound is called *schwa*. It is made by relaxing your tongue in the middle of your mouth. It sounds like "uh."

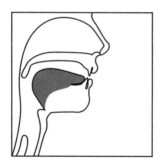

The /ə/ sound occurs in most unstressed syllables. It also occurs in some stressed syllables in such words as *bug, money,* and *stuff.* In this lesson, you will practice /ə/ only in unstressed syllables.

Predict the /ə/ Sound in Words

Each of the following words from Jill's conversation has at least one /ə/ sound. Underline the syllable(s) where you expect to hear this sound. Remember, this sound occurs in many, but not all, unstressed syllables.

Example: <u>a</u>partm<u>e</u>nt

1. garden
2. office
3. about
4. maintenance
5. repaired

6. today
7. appliance
8. tonight
9. away
10. immediately

Practice the /ə/ Sound in Words

Listen again, and underline the syllables that have the /ə/ sound. Then, compare your answers with your predictions.

Example: <u>a</u>partm<u>e</u>nt

1. garden
2. office
3. about
4. maintenance
5. repaired

6. today
7. appliance
8. tonight
9. away
10. immediately

Listen to the words again. Repeat each after the speaker. Practice the correct pronunciation of /ə/.

Practice the /ə/ Sound in Sentences

In the following sentences from the conversation, mark the vowels that are pronounced /ə/. Then, listen to the tape, and repeat after the speaker. Practice the correct pronunciation of /ə/.

1. Hello, Garden Apartment's Maintenance Office.

2. This is Jill Portman from apartment 30B.

3. I need to have the stove repaired today.

4. He does the appliance repairs.

5. Well, I hope you can get it fixed immediately.

Practice Pronouncing the /ə/ Sound

Student A: Check **one** word in each of the following pairs. Do not tell Student B which word you checked. Read it to your partner.

Student B: Listen to the word that your partner reads. In the following pairs, check the sentence that contains this word.

After you have completed all six items, compare your answers. Then switch roles and repeat the exercise.

1. ____ **RE**cord   ____ It is hard to buy records now; CDs are more popular.

    ____ re**CORD**   ____ The teacher asked us to record our voices on tape.

2. ____ **IN**crease   ____ The workers want a salary increase.

    ____ in**CREASE**   ____ The temperature increases every summer.

3. ____ **PRE**sent   ____ Everyone in our class is present today.

    ____ pre**SENT**   ____ The students presented their teacher with a birthday card.

4. ____ **PRO**gress   ____ The students are making good progress.

    ____ pro**GRESS**   ____ When everyone participates, class progresses quickly.

5. ____ **PRO**ject   ____ They are working on a class project together.

    ____ pro**JECT**   ____ I need to project the overhead onto the screen.

6. ____ **CON**flict   ____ I can't take that class because of a time conflict.

    ____ con**FLICT**   ____ That class conflicts with my work schedule.

On Your Own

List six common words whose word stress confuses you. Check the correct word stress with your teacher, a dictionary, or friends. Practice your list each day on your own, with a partner, or on tape until you can say the words correctly without thinking about their pronunciations.

1. _____   4. _____

2. _____   5. _____

3. _____   6. _____

TALK It Up!

Getting Things Fixed

When you need to have something repaired, you need to give the person doing the repair some important information. You also need to ask some important questions. Be sure to tell the repair person what the problem is:

- The burners on my stove won't get hot.
- The toilet isn't flushing properly.

Also tell the repair person how often the problem occurs or under what circumstances:

- The television picture goes blank after the television has been on for 10 minutes.
- There is no hot water in my bathroom in the morning.

Make sure that you find out when the person will fix the problem:

- When can I bring my TV to your shop?
- When will you come to my house?
- How long will the repairs take?

Also, find out how much the repairs will cost:

- Can you give me an estimate? The repairs won't cost more than the estimate, right?
- You will bill my landlord for these repairs, right?
- Is it more expensive to repair or to replace this appliance?

Be sure to get the answers about the cost or timeliness of repairs before the repairs are begun.

   Note: It is usually the landlord's responsibility to make repairs in appliances that come with a rented apartment. Check your lease to see which repairs are the landlord's responsibility and which repairs might be your responsibility.

Complete the following chart about whom you should call when something breaks.

Appliance/ Equipment	Problem	Professional to Call for Repair	Person Responsible
Stove	The oven won't get hot.	Appliance repair person	The landlord
	The water won't go out after it is done washing.	Appliance repair person	
Plumbing	The shower/sink leaks, (or) the toilet won't flush.		
Refrigerator		Refrigerator repair person	
TV or VCR			
Vacuum cleaner	It won't pick up dirt, (or) no air moves through the hose.		
	The house is too cold.	Heating contractor and service person	
Air conditioning		Air conditioning contractor and maintenance person	

Role-Playing

With a partner, use the previous chart to role-play a conversation with a landlord or a repairperson. Be creative! For example, one partner could be angry, afraid, or uncooperative.

Another Way to Role-Play

Choose several people to play the role of professionals. Each of these people chooses one of the professions from the previous chart. They then sit near a sign that tells his or her profession. The rest of the group then visits each professional to talk about having something fixed. Be sure to visit the right professional!

Listening Three
What a Neighborhood!

You will hear three people talking about things that they like and things that they don't like about the neighborhood in which they live. You might not understand every word that is said the first time that you listen. That's all right. Focus on what you do understand. You will have opportunities to discuss the information and listen again.

Before You Listen

How do you describe the neighborhood in which you live? Write three things that you like about your neighborhood and three things you don't like about it.

Things that I like   Things that I don't like

_____   _____

_____   _____

_____   _____

_____   _____

_____   _____

_____   _____

Discuss your list in pairs or in a small group to find out if others said similar things about their neighborhoods.

Listen for Attitudes

 Listen to these people talk about their neighborhood. Finish each of the following sentences with one word or phrase that describes each person's attitude about this neighborhood.

1. The first man interviewed says the neighborhood is

    _____.

2. The single mom is concerned about

    _____.

3. The third person interviewed thinks that the neighborhood is

    _____.

Take Notes

 Listen to the interview again, taking notes in the following chart as you listen.

TALKING POINT

Taking notes helps you to be a better listener because to do so, you must focus on important information.

	What does he or she like about the neighborhood?	What does he or she dislike about the neighborhood?
First Speaker		
Second Speaker		
Third Speaker		

With a partner or on tape, use the notes that you took to describe the neighborhood at Park Street and Princess Avenue. Include as many details as you can in your description. Listen to your recording to check your pronunciation of word stress.

After You Listen

Two of the people interviewed tell something about themselves and then they tell why this makes the neighborhood good or bad for them. For example:

1. I'm a single mom, so safety is important to me.

2. I'm a night owl, so I kind of wish there were some interesting places open at night.

What would you say if you had to describe yourself in a few words, and explain why you chose the home or neighborhood that you did.

_____

_____

_____

_____

Share your self-description with a partner or small group.

Further Practice

Self-Evaluation

Go back to the pronunciation and fluency test record in the preface.
Record the test a second time, using the following paragraph and picture.
Listen to your recording. What errors can you find? Re-record any words or
phrases that you mispronounced, trying to correct your mistakes. Then,
with your teacher's help, answer the following questions.

1. What has improved?

_____

2. What will you work on next?

_____

Record the results of your self-evaluation in the chart on page xviii in the
preface.

Etiquette for Dinner Guests

What would you do if you received an invitation to a friend's house for dinner? Would you take a gift? Would you take food or drink to share with the hosts? Usually, when you are invited to a dinner party in Canada or the United States, you are not expected to take a present. However, if you want to present the hosts with a small gift like flowers or a souvenir to show your thanks, it surely will be accepted and appreciated. Guests often call the host before the day of the dinner and ask, "Is there anything I can bring?" Sometimes the host will suggest that the guest bring a dessert or a bottle of wine. If you don't drink alcoholic beverages, it is polite to say so and to ask if you could bring dessert instead. At some dinner parties, guests prepare some kind of food to share. These get-togethers are called "potluck" dinners. Usually the host provides the main dish, and guests choose to bring a vegetable, salad, or dessert dish for everyone to enjoy.

Class Project: Give an Oral Presentation

Describing Your Neighborhood

What are the best things about your neighborhood? What do you wish were different? Based on what you have heard and talked about in this unit, prepare a short presentation about your home or neighborhood. Share this presentation with a small group of classmates or the entire class. Do not write the entire presentation and read from this script; it is boring for the audience. Instead, follow these presentation tips.

1. Make a few notes using the following form.

    a. Introduction: Where is your home or neighborhood?

    _____

    _____

    Give a brief description of your home or neighborhood.

    _____

    _____

    b. What do you like about your home or neighborhood?

    _____

    _____

    c. What do you wish were different about your home or neighborhood?

    _____

d.   Would you recommend that other people move to your neighborhood or a home like yours? Why?

_____

_____

2.   Transfer your notes to note cards.

3.   Practice your presentation until you can speak easily without looking too long at the cards.

4.   Use the note cards to give a short presentation to a small group or the class.

5.   Your teacher or your classmates will give you feedback using the following chart. Use this chart for future presentations as well.

Feedback Form for Oral Presentations

Topic	4 = Excellent	3 = Good	2 = Average	1 = Needs Improvement
Content: Amount of information				
Content: Clearly organized				
Speaking: Clarity				
Speaking: Pronunciation				
Speaking: Stress and intonation				
Speaking: Volume				
Speaking: Body language and eye contact				
Comments:				

3

Making Connections

CHAPTER HIGHLIGHTS

Listening	Pronunciation	Speaking	Class Project
Listen for main ideas Listen for step-by-step order Listen for details Listen for specific information	/ey/, /ɛ/, and /æ/ Contractions	Give step-by-step explanations Express sympathy Listen and respond Make a telephone chain	Phrases for signing greeting cards

Brainstorming

Communication Choices

The following pictures show some ways that people communicate with each other. Match each person in the list that follows with the ways in which you have communicated with that person.

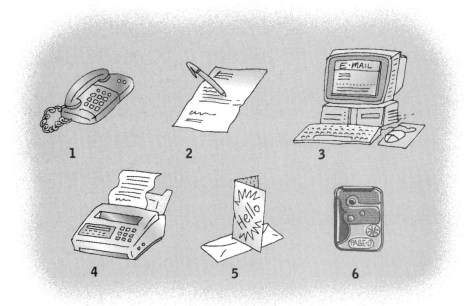

People with whom to communicate:

_1, 2_ mother   _____ spouse (husband or wife)

_____ casual friends   _____ coworkers

_____ father   _____ best friends

_____ teachers   _____ a boyfriend or girlfriend

_____ siblings (brothers and sisters)   _____ business partner

_____ grandparents   _____ classmates

With a partner or in a small group, explain your choices. Talk about the advantages and disadvantages of each type of communication.

Listening One
E-Mail Connections

Victor has a paper due at noon today. The paper is finished, but his car won't start, so he can't take the paper to turn it in. He calls his friend Leslie to ask for her help.

Listen for Main Ideas

Read the following list of solutions to Victor's problem. Then listen to the conversation and write the letter V next to the way in which Victor wants to solve the problem. Write the letter L next to the way in which Leslie wants to solve the problem.

_____ Call the professor and ask for an extension.

_____ Ask a friend to drive him to school.

_____ Get the car fixed.

_____ Send the paper from Leslie's computer.

_____ Send the paper in the mail.

_____ Take the bus to school.

Listen for Step-by-Step Order

Leslie suggests several steps that Victor must take to solve his problem. Listen to the conversation again, and number the following steps in the order in which Leslie suggests them.

_____ Take the disk to Leslie's house.

_1_ Call the professor.

_____ Save the paper on disk.

_____ Send the paper from Leslie's computer.

_____ Get the professor's e-mail address.

After You Listen

Imagine that you are Victor, and the problem has been solved. Using the past tense, retell in detail the story of what happened and how you solved the problem.

Pronunciation ACTIVITIES

/ey/ as in play, /ɛ/ as in send, and /æ/ as in bad

You make these three vowel sounds by placing your tongue in the front of your mouth.

- Make /ey/ by placing your tongue in the middle and front of the mouth. At the end of the /ey/ sound is a /y/ sound. To make this sound, you move your jaw and tongue up a little bit. The words *make, stay,* and *paper* have this sound.

- /ɛ/ is a lower than /ey/, but higher and shorter than /æ/. Make the /ey/ sound but don't pronounce the /y/ sound at the end. Then lower your tongue and drop your jaw a little bit to make the /ɛ/ sound. The words *letter, bed,* and *fell* all have this sound.

- /æ/ is a lower, longer vowel sound. When you make this sound, your tongue must be very low. Your jaw will even drop a little. You must stretch your lips slightly to say /æ/. The words *happy, plan,* and *mad* have this sound.

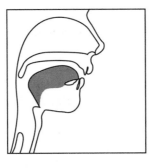 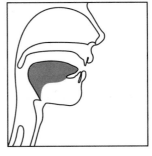 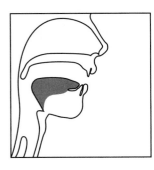

pl<u>ay</u>   s<u>e</u>nd   b<u>a</u>d

Try to make these vowel sounds correctly in the following words:

mate /ey/	met /ɛ/	mat /æ/
pain /ey/	pen /ɛ/	pan /æ/

Practice /ey/, /ɛ/, and /æ/ in Words

Each of the following words from the conversation has one of the sounds /ey/, /ɛ/, or /æ/. Underline the sound that you predict that you will hear. Then listen to the conversation and for each word circle the sound that you hear.

1. paper   /ey/   /ɛ/   /æ/
2. classes   /ey/   /ɛ/   /æ/
3. ask   /ey/   /ɛ/   /æ/
4. send   /ey/   /ɛ/   /æ/
5. rest   /ey/   /ɛ/   /æ/
6. century   /ey/   /ɛ/   /æ/
7. save   /ey/   /ɛ/   /æ/
8. place   /ey/   /ɛ/   /æ/
9. great   /ey/   /ɛ/   /æ/
10. crash   /ey/   /ɛ/   /æ/

Listen again, repeating each of these words after the speaker. Look at them to see some ways that /ey/, /ɛ/, and /æ/ can be spelled.

Practice /ey/, /ɛ/, and /æ/ in Sentences

In the following sentences from the conversation, find the words that have the /ey/, /ɛ/, and /æ/ sounds. Then listen to the sentences, repeating each after the speaker says it and practice saying /ey/, /ɛ/, and /æ/ correctly.

1. I've got this paper due for one of my classes.

2. Can you send the paper by e-mail?

3. Someday you'll have to join the rest of us in the twenty-first century.

4. Next, save your paper on disk.

5. Bring the disk and the e-mail address over here to my place.

Practice Pronouncing /ey/, /ɛ/, and /æ/

Student A: Mark **one** word in each of the following pairs. Do not tell Student B which word you chose. Read the word to your partner.

Student B: Check the sentence that has the word that your partner read.

After you and your partner have completed all eight items, compare answers. Then, reverse roles and repeat the exercise.

1. ____ sat   ____ I sat in the first seat.
   ____ set   ____ I set the glass on the table.

2. ____ men   ____ I saw three men.
   ____ man   ____ I saw one man.

3. ____ laughed   ____ She laughed at the joke.
   ____ left   ____ She left after class.

4. ____ pan   ____ A pan is used for cooking.
   ____ pen   ____ A pen is used for writing.

5. ____ paper   ____ I need paper to write a letter.
   ____ pepper   ____ Please pass the salt and pepper.

6. ____ plane   ____ We're going to take a plane.
   ____ plan   ____ You should make a plan first.

7. ____ test   ____ How did you do on the test?
   ____ taste   ____ I want to taste the cookies.

8. ____ made   ____ We made the cake ourselves.
   ____ mad   ____ His father was really mad.

TALKING POINT

If the words that you marked matched the answers that your partner marked, you both probably pronounced and heard the sounds correctly. If the markings do not match, you and your partner should repeat these exercises. If you need help, ask your teacher.

Communicative Pronunciation Practice

Fill in the following sentences using any words from the lists provided.

Name		Verb	Method of Communication	
Angie	Abraham	sends	letters	packages
Fred	James	mails	aerograms	express mail
Jennifer	Andy		faxes	telegrams
Amy	Traci		e-mail	

Name	Verb	Method of Communication	
Angie	_sends_	_telegrams_	to her grandfather.
_____	_____	_____	to his or her family.
_____	_____	_____	to his or her professor.
_____	_____	_____	to his or her best friend.
_____	_____	_____	to his or her classmate.

Mark the /ey/, /ɛ/, and /æ/ sounds in your sentences.

Take turns with a partner saying what you both wrote. Write your partner's sentences in the following spaces and then repeat them to your partner to be sure that you understood. As you speak, practice pronouncing the /ey/, /ɛ/, and /æ/ sounds correctly.

Name	Verb	Method of Communication	
Angie	_sends_	_telegrams_	to her grandfather.
_____	_____	_____	to his or her family.
_____	_____	_____	to his or her professor.
_____	_____	_____	to his or her best friend.
_____	_____	_____	to his or her classmate.

On Your Own

Make a list of words that you use every day that have the vowel sounds you just practiced. (Be sure to add the names of places in the town where you live!) Study this list often, and try to pronounce the words correctly every time that you use them.

/ey/ _____

/ɛ/ _____

/æ/ _____

TALK It Up!

Step-by-Step Explanations

In the conversation in this section, Leslie uses organizing words such as *first, then,* and *next* to help Victor understand how she thinks he should solve his problem. These words help to mark the steps in a process.

Here are some other organizing words that help make the steps in a story or a solution to a problem clear:

first	next	the last thing is
second	then	finally
third	the next step is	last

Use these words whenever you are explaining how to do something so that your listener will better understand each step.

Practice Using Step-by-Step Explanations

Choose one of the following problems, and then on the lines that follow, write in note form possible solutions to the problem.

1. You lost your house keys and can't get into your house.

2. You forgot your glasses at a concert.

3. You locked your keys in your car.

4. You are at the grocery store waiting in line to pay when you realize that you left your checkbook and wallet at home.

Possible solutions:

_____

_____

_____

_____

Discuss with others in your class the problem that you chose. Use organizing words to explain the steps that you would take to solve the problem.

Listening Two
Send a Card to Stay in Touch

Vanessa is in a gift shop buying some greeting cards. She sees her friend Kelly. They talk about the greeting cards that they are buying.

Before You Listen

People often make telephone calls, send greeting cards, or send e-mail greetings to each other on special occasions. In the following list, match each occasion on the left with the kind of greeting that you would send on the right. Explain your choices to others in your class.

_____ a birthday   _____ a. a greeting card

_____ a wedding   _____ b. a telephone call

_____ a funeral   _____ c. an e-mail greeting

_____ to thank someone   _____ d. other: _____

_____ when someone is sick

Listen for Main Ideas

 Listen to the conversation, and check in the following list the kinds of greeting cards that Vanessa and Kelly are buying.

Kelly   Vanessa

_____ a birthday card   _____ a birthday card

_____ a thank-you card   _____ a thank-you card

_____ a sympathy card   _____ a sympathy card

_____ a get well card   _____ a get well card

Listen for Details

Listen to the conversation again to hear the answers to the following questions.

1. What problem does Vanessa have with her gifts?
    a. The gifts are the wrong size.
    b. She doesn't like the gifts very much.
    c. She got two presents from one person.
    d. Both (b) and (c).

2. How does Vanessa plan to solve the problem?
    a. She will ask her grandmother and aunt to buy her a new present.
    b. She will send her grandmother and aunt thank-you cards.
    c. She will ask her mother to tell her relatives that she did not like the gifts.
    d. Both (b) and (c).

After You Listen

If you were Vanessa, what would you do if a friend or relative sent you a gift that you did not like? Mark your choice in the following list. Discuss your solution with others in your class, and explain what you think the gift-giver's reaction would be.

_____ Ask for the receipt so that you can return the gift and choose another.

_____ Thank the person for the gift, and tell him or her that you like it. (Tell a white lie.)

_____ Thank the person for the gift but do not say that you liked it.

_____ Ask another friend or relative to find out if the gift can be returned or exchanged.

_____ Do nothing.

_____ Other: _____

Using one of these solutions, role-play with a partner a conversation in which Vanessa's problem is solved.

Pronunciation ACTIVITIES

Contractions

Contractions are very common in spoken English. A contraction is made when two words are pronounced as one. Contractions of pronouns and auxiliary verbs are common in informal written English.

Be Verbs

I am	=	I'm	We are	=	We're
He is	=	He's	You are	=	You're
She is	=	She's	They are	=	They're
It is	=	It's			

Will

I'll	You'll	He'll	She'll	We'll	They'll

Have/Has

I've	You've	He's	She's	We've	They've

Not

Not also is commonly written as part of a contraction:

isn't   aren't   wasn't   weren't   can't   don't

Contractions are written only with pronouns and never with nouns. When we speak, the following auxiliary verbs often sound contracted even though they follow a noun and not a pronoun.

Are almost always sounds contracted.
    These children're very good students.
    The students're doing their homework right now.

Will almost always sounds contracted.
    The sun'll come out tomorrow.
    I know my friend'll remember my birthday.

Would and *had* both sound contracted as a /d/ sound.
    I would have helped you if you had asked. =
    I'd have helped you if you'd asked.

Has and *is* both sound like /s/ when contracted.

The bus has already come.	=	The bus's already come.
Clara is always late.	=	Clara's always late.

Practice Hearing Contractions

 In the following sentences, the contracted words are missing. Listen to the phrases and write in the spaces the two words that are contracted.

1. _____ _____ you been up to?

2. _____ _____ looking for a condolence card.

3. It's important he knows _____ _____ thinking about him.

4. I _____ _____ believe it!

5. _____ _____ weird!

6. They _____ _____ thought _____ _____ like it.

7. Maybe I _____ _____ when I was sixteen.

8. _____ _____ not my style now.

9. I _____ _____ want to hurt their feelings.

10. _____ _____ ask my mom.

Listen again, repeating each contraction after the speaker says it. Try to make contractions with the words in the same way that the speaker does.

Practice Pronouncing Contractions

The following paragraph is missing words that are pronounced as contractions. With a partner, take turns reading the paragraph from page 169, pronouncing the missing words as contractions. As your partner reads the paragraph, fill in the long form of the contracted words.

Meeting People and Making Friends

When you move to a new town or start a new school, you might find it hard to meet people. Some people _____ _____ learning English feel even more nervous because they worry about their English speaking abilities. If _____ _____ like to meet people and you _____ _____ had any success, _____ _____ got some suggestions. One of the easiest ways to meet people and make _____ _____ to introduce yourself to the people around you. Talk to your neighbors when _____ _____ coming home, or ask people at school or work about themselves. You might find out _____ _____ liked_____ _____ talked to you sooner if _____ _____ known how to start the conversation. If _____ _____ like to meet people other than those whom you see everyday, why not join a club _____ _____ interested in? _____ _____ be lots of people there _____ _____ be interested in the same thing. You could also volunteer your time at a local charity or children's program. _____ _____ a great way to meet people. Meeting people _____ _____ always easy, and _____ _____ take some time and effort, but _____ _____ probably find _____ _____ happy and willing to get to know you.

On the following lines, write five sentences about meeting new people. Underline all of the words that can be contracted.

1. _____

2. _____

3. _____

4. _____

5. _____

Read the sentences, contracting the underlined words. To check your pronunciation, rewrite the sentences with blanks where the contractions should be and read to a partner who fills in the blanks. Or, record yourself reading the sentences with contractions.

TALK It Up!

Expressing Sympathy

Sometimes we learn that something unfortunate or sad has happened to a friend. It is often difficult to know what to say to this person because you do not want to make your friend uncomfortable by reminding him or her about it. However, saying nothing is also uncomfortable and might make you seem insensitive.

If you heard about the unfortunate situation from someone else, you could say, for example:

- I heard that you and your family are having some difficult times. I'm sorry to hear about that.
- I was sorry to hear about your misfortune.

If your friend tells you about the problem, you could say, for example:

- That's really too bad.
- I'm very sorry to hear that.

It also is usually a good idea to let the person know that you care and would like to help, for example:

- How are you doing now? Are you OK?
- Let me know if there's anything that I can do to help.

If people do not want to talk about something unfortunate, they usually give a short response, such as "thank you," and then change the subject. If this happens, it is best not to talk about the problem further.

For each of the following difficult social situations, write on the lines two possible answers that you would say.

1. A friend was in a car accident, and her car was badly damaged.

   _____
   _____

2. A good friend lost her job.

   _____
   _____

3. A friend's father, who had been very sick, passed away.

   _____
   _____

Share your answers with others in your class. How would you communicate these messages? By e-mail, greeting card, letter, telephone, or some other method? Explain your choices.

Role-Playing

With a partner, role-play a conversation about one of these three situations. Be prepared to present your role-play to others in the class. Plan what you will say together, but do not write your lines word for word; you do not need to memorize your part.

Listening Three
Not Another Answering Machine!

Before You Listen

Answer the following questions to yourself. Then share your answers with a partner or a small group of classmates.

1. When you call someone and you get voice mail, do you usually leave a message? Why or why not?

2. What information should a voice mail greeting give?

In the following list, draw a line through any information or phrases that *should not* be in a voice mail greeting. Be prepared to explain your choices.

Your name

Your telephone number

"I'm not home right now."

A date or time when you will be home

"Leave a message after the tone."

"I'll call you back as soon as I can."

Listen for Specific Information

Kelly is calling several of her friends. Not many people are home, so she has to leave messages on answering machines.

Look at Kelly's telephone number list, and then listen to each call to hear whom she is calling. Number, next to the name, the first person that she calls, the second person that she calls, and so on.

Brad	555-3454
Molly	555-7687
Chad	555-6666
Andre	555-3444
Lara	555-0990

Listen for Details

Listen again, and then circle the correct answer to the following statements.

1. Brad cannot answer the phone because he is on vacation.

   True   False   Not enough information given

2. When Lara says, "You know what to do now!" she means, "Call back later."

   True   False   Not enough information given

3. One message has no name. It is probably a wrong number.

   True   False   Not enough information given

4. Jason, Andre, and Marc's message is funny because the machine sounds like a real person.

   True   False   Not enough information given

5. When Kelly made the fifth call, she got another answering machine.

   True   False   Not enough information given

Listen and Respond

If you were Kelly, what message would you leave on your friends' machines? Would you leave the same message on all machines or make each message a little different?

Look at the following information about Kelly's party. Listen to the answering-machine messages again. After each message, pause the recording and leave an answering-machine message about the party.

After You Listen

Make an answering-machine greeting like the ones that Kelly heard when she called her friends. You may make a typical message or an original, funny one that suits your personality. You can do this activity on paper in the classroom or on tape in a language lab (if one is available).

Just for Fun!

Have an answering-machine message contest. Imagine that you cannot
come to class. On tape, in the language lab, or on paper, create an answering-machine message that explains why you must be absent. The class will
listen to all of the messages (in the lab or as a whole), and vote on which
message is the following:

1. funniest

2. craziest

3. most direct

4. most unlikely to be true

5. other: _____

Telephone Chain

Make a telephone chain in your class by following these steps:

1. Each student writes his or her name and telephone number on a sheet
   of paper.

2. Each student receives a copy of this telephone list.

3. The teacher calls the student at the top of the list and gives him or her
   a secret message.

4. That student calls the next student on the list and passes on the
   message.

5. The second student calls the third, and so on.

   If the chain works properly, the last student on the list should be able
to tell the class the correct message. (If your class is large, several smaller
telephone chains can be made.)

Further Practice

Class Project: Phrases for Signing Greeting Cards

Collect phrases that people write in greeting cards, and add these phrases to the following list. In a group, discuss these phrases. Would you write a similar or different phrase in other languages that you speak?

For someone's birthday:

Wishing you a happy birthday and many more to come!
Wishing you happiness in the coming year!

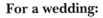

For a wedding:

Good luck for your future together!
Wishing you all the best!

For someone who is sick:

Get well soon!
I am thinking about you.

For the death of someone's friend or relative:

You have my deepest sympathy.
Please accept my condolences.

For the birth of a baby:

Congratulations on the birth of your child.
Good luck to you and your new baby.

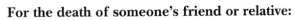

For a holiday:

Have a happy (New Year's Day, St. Patrick's Day, Christmas, and so on)

Interview a Fellow Student

Find out how other students in your class or your school communicate with family, friends, and others by interviewing three people. Before you begin, review the interviewing tips on pages 7–9 in Chapter 1.

1. In a small group, think of at least five questions that could be asked during the interview.

2. Write three of those questions in the following Interviewing Chart.

3. Interview three people, and note their answers in the Interviewing Chart.

Interviewing Chart

Your Questions	First Person's Answers	Second Person's Answers	Third Person's Answers

4. In a small group, report on the results of your interview and then summarize your group's discussion for the class.

4

The World of Work

CHAPTER HIGHLIGHTS

Listening	Pronunciation	Speaking	Class Project
Get the gist	/iy/ and /ɪ/	Listen and respond	Talk to an expert
Listen for implied meaning	Sentence stress	Conduct formal interviews	
Listen for main ideas		Start a conversation and keep it going	
Listen for details			
Take notes			

Brainstorming

Characteristics That Help on the Job

The following is a list of characteristics that help people do their jobs well. With a group of classmates, write on the lines a job that requires each of these characteristics. Then for each, give a job that does not require these characteristics.

	Job that requires this characteristic	Job that does not require this characteristic
Gets along well with people	_____	_____
Works well with his/her hands	_____	_____
Organized	_____	_____
Very patient	_____	_____
Likes excitement	_____	_____
Creative	_____	_____
Likes to build and fix things	_____	_____
Enjoys math and science	_____	_____
Physically strong	_____	_____
Has good problem-solving skills	_____	_____
Able to meet deadlines	_____	_____
Works well under pressure	_____	_____

With a new partner or in a new group, compare your lists and explain your choices.

Listening One
Getting the Job

In a job interview, the interviewer asks questions to see whether you are the right person to get the work done. At the interview, you want to show that you are the best person for the job, and you get a chance to ask questions to find out if the job and the company are right for you.

Before You Listen

Read the following job interview questions. Mark the three questions that you think would be most important to ask if you were interviewing some-one for a part-time administrative job.

_____ What are your greatest strengths?

_____ What is one of your weaknesses?

_____ What is your educational background?

_____ What did you like about your previous job?

_____ Why did you leave your previous job?

_____ Why do you want to work here?

Explain your choices to others in your class.

Listen to Get the Gist

Connie Yablonsky is a graphic designer who is interviewing for a job at a company called Impressions Advertising. Her interview with Ms. Thompson, a manager at Impressions, will be about 25 minutes long. You will listen to just one part of the interview.

 Listen to the interview. Then, in the following list, mark each kind of information that Connie gives about her background and experience.

_____ her previous work experience

_____ the languages that she speaks

_____ her personal characteristics

_____ her interpersonal skills

_____ the salary that she expects

_____ her educational background

_____ her ability to work in teams

_____ her future career plans

Listen for Implied Meaning

In this interview, Connie's answers imply something about her skills, abilities, and experience and how those will affect her work if she is hired. To *imply* means to say something indirectly. In an interview, people say positive things about themselves indirectly. This allows them to make a positive impression on the interviewer without appearing rude or self-centered.

Listen to Connie's answers and decide what each answer implies.

1. Connie tells Ms. Thompson why she wants to leave her present job. What does her answer imply?
   a. Connie is hard working.
   b. Connie is responsible.
   c. Connie is creative.
   d. Connie is a team player.

2. Connie talks about the characteristics that she has that make her a good designer. What does her answer imply?
   a. She is talented and her coworkers can learn a lot from her.
   b. She wants to design newspapers at Impressions.
   c. She is creative and experienced.
   d. She is a good psychologist.

3. Connie describes the contributions that she could make to Impressions. What does her answer imply?
   a. She likes to work with others.
   b. She understands the importance of deadlines.
   c. She uses computers well.
   d. She wants to be more creative than her boss.

4. Connie asks a question at the end of the interview. What does her question imply?
   a. She wants the job.
   b. She wants to work in groups.
   c. She is a good leader as well as a talented designer.
   d. She is interested in knowing what the job is like.

Listen and Respond

Listen to the beginning of this conversation, and when the recording stops, finish the conversation with a partner. Your conversation may end differently from Connie and Ms. Thompson's or in the same way. Be prepared to share your ending with the class.

Pronunciation ACTIVITIES

/iy/ **as in seen and** /ɪ/ **as in did**

These two vowel sounds are made by raising your tongue high in the front of your mouth.

- /iy/ is a higher and longer vowel sound than is /ɪ/. When you make this sound, your tongue must be very high and your lips must be stretched. Try to smile a little when you say /iy/. That is why people say, "Say cheese!" when they take a picture. The /iy/ sound in cheese makes you smile.
- /ɪ/ is a little lower, shorter, and more relaxed than is /iy/. Make the /iy/ sound, but do not add the /y/ sound at the end, and lower your tongue slightly and relax your lips to make the /ɪ/ sound. The words *sit*, *middle*, and *mister* have this sound.

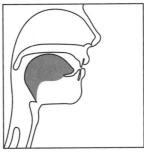

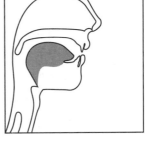

seen   did

Try to make both sounds in these word pairs:

       seat /iy/   sit /ɪ/

       feel /iy/   fill /ɪ/

Practice /iy/ **and** /ɪ/ **in Words**

The following words from the conversation have either an / iy / or an / ɪ / sound. Predict which sound you will hear, and then listen and circle the sound that you hear.

1. see	/iy/ /ɪ/		6. skills	/iy/ /ɪ/
2. interesting	/iy/ /ɪ/		7. contribute	/iy/ /ɪ/
3. responsibility	/iy/ /ɪ/		8. believe	/iy/ /ɪ/
4. characteristics	/iy/ /ɪ/		9. team	/iy/ /ɪ/
5. people	/iy/ /ɪ/		10. each	/iy/ /ɪ/

Listen to the words again, and repeat each after the speaker. Look at them to see some ways that /iy/ and /ɪ/ can be spelled.

Practice /iy/ and /ɪ/ in Sentences

 Listen to the following sentences, from the conversation, that contain words that have the /iy/ and /ɪ/ sounds. Repeat each sentence after the speaker, practicing the correct pronunciation of /iy/ and /ɪ/.

1. You'd have a lot of responsibility here.

2. I think a designer has to understand people, too.

3. What else can you contribute to Impressions?

4. And I believe in creative leadership.

5. Each of our projects has a creative team, and on the larger projects there are several designers.

Practice Pronouncing /iy/ and /ɪ/

Student A: Check **one** sentence in each of the following pairs. Do not tell Student B which sentence you checked. Read it to Student B.

Student B: Listen to the sentence that your partner reads. Check the appropriate response.

After you and your partner have completed all six items, compare your answers. Then reverse roles and repeat the exercise.

1. ____ He beat me again!   ____ He always wins when we play cards.

    ____ He bit me again!   ____ I must take my dog to training school.

2. ____ He has to leave   ____ before midnight.

    ____ He has to live   ____ with his parents to save money.

3. ____ It was the hit   ____ song on the album.

    ____ It was the heat   ____ that made him feel sick.

4. ____ I gave the boy a toy ship   ____ because he likes boats.

    ____ I gave the boy a toy sheep ____ because he likes animals.

5.   ____ Fill the glass.   ____ I'm really thirsty.

     ____ Feel the glass.   ____ It's smooth.

6.   ____ He had a green   ____ car.

     ____ He had a grin   ____ on his face.

Communicative Pronunciation Practice

With a partner, complete the following chart.

Student A: Look at this page.

Student B: Look at page 170 at the end of the book.

Ask each other questions to find out which people have the same occupation. Be sure to pronounce /iy/ and /ɪ/ correctly.

Example: A: What does Lynn do?

               B: She's a business executive.

               A: OK. So is Nicky.

TALKING POINT

The names and occupations in the chart contain /iy/ and /ɪ/ sounds.
You may mark the symbols above the words before you begin to help you to
practice pronouncing these sounds correctly.

Lynn: Business executive	Elizabeth: Housecleaner	Rick: Teacher	Linda: Electrician
Tina: Administrative assistant	Leo: Physical therapist	Gene: Nutritionist	Trena: Engineer
Bill: 1. _____	Jim: 2. _____	Nicky: 3. _____	Tim: 4. _____
Peter: 5. _____	Rita: 6. _____	Lisa: 7. _____	Steve: 8. _____

On Your Own

Make a list of words that you use every day that use the vowel sounds you have just practiced. (Be sure to add the names of places in a city or town where you live!) Study this list often, and try to pronounce the words correctly every time that you use them.

/iy/ _____

/ɪ/ _____

TALK It Up!

Formal Interviews

In earlier chapters, you practiced planning questions to ask others in an interview. Sometimes, however, you might find that you are the interviewee, and you must answer questions. Before any interview, you should think about the questions that you might be asked. Here are some topics that are typical in interviews.

A job or scholarship interview:

- your education
- your work experience
- your personal characteristics

A less formal interview (for example, with a potential student at your school or for an opinion poll):

- your personal experiences
- your thoughts about a current issue

Once you have thought about the questions that you will be asked, you should plan good answers to these questions. Here are some tips to help you give good answers in personal interviews.

- Give positive answers.
- Answer specifically. Give details and examples to make your answers clear.
- Focus on your accomplishments and the things that you have done.
- Answer directly.

Practice Predicting Interview Questions

With a partner or in a group, list three questions that an interviewer might ask in each of the following types of interview. Then, in the last space on the following Interviewing Chart, add another type of interview and write questions for this type of interview.

Interviewing Chart

Type of Interview	Question
A job interview	
An interview for a scholarship	
An interview for the college newspaper or about a club you belong to	
Another kind of interview: _____	

Answer Interview Questions

Which of the following answers will help you to get across your best qualities? Which do not make a good impression? Remembering the tips for answering interview questions, try to improve the answer for each question.

1. Q.   Why would you like to do this job?
   A.   The high salary you are paying is what really attracted me to this position.
   Improved Answer:

   _____

2. Q.   Which of your achievements are you most proud of?
   A.   I don't know. I can't think of one. I've done lots of things.
   Improved Answer:

   _____

3. Q.   Why should I hire you?

   A.   Well, I have a lot of experience working with people, and I speak three languages, so I could help the company do international business.

   Improved Answer:

   _____

4. Q.   Your resume doesn't show a lot of experience working with computers. I need someone who works well with computers. Could you work well with computers?

   A.   I don't really like computers very much. I prefer to use a type-writer.

   Improved Answer:

   _____

5. Q.   Tell me about the special programs that your group sponsors.

   A.   We hold at least one special event each month. For example, just last month we had an amateur music festival and we awarded prizes from local businesses.

   Improved Answer:

   _____

Compare your choices with a partner's. Try to agree on your answers, and then present the results to others in the class.

Role-Playing

With a partner, choose a type of interview from the previous Interviewing Chart. Use what you have learned about interviews to plan your role-play.

Student A: You are the interviewer.

Student B: You are the interviewee.

Then, change roles. Be prepared to present your role-plays to others in the class.

Listening Two
Breaking the Ice

Connie got the job at Impressions and is having lunch at a nearby cafe on her first week of work. In the cafe, she sees Ken, a coworker, and decides to start a conversation with him.

Before You Listen

Put a check mark next to topics that people who do not know each other well can talk about in your first language.

_____	the weather	_____	religion
_____	your salaries	_____	current events
_____	your families	_____	sports
_____	your ages	_____	clothing that you are
_____	your health		wearing
_____	food/meals	_____	your occupations

Compare your answers with a partner's. Explain the reasons for your choices.

   With a partner, brainstorm a list of questions about what you can talk about in English when you first meet someone.

Listen for Main Ideas

Listen to Connie and Ken's conversation, and check the topics that they talk about.

_____	their jobs	_____	things to do for fun
_____	their salaries	_____	current events
_____	their boss	_____	sports

Listen for Details

Listen again, and answer the following questions.

1. How does Connie begin her conversation with Ken?

   _____

   _____

2. What is Connie's first impression about her new workplace?

   _____

   _____

3. What advantages of working for Impressions does Ken describe?

   _____

   _____

4. What do the coworkers at Impressions do each month?

   _____

   _____

5. Why does Connie not know what there is to do in this community?

   _____

   _____

After You Listen

Choose one or more of the following activities.

1. With your class, discuss what Connie and Ken might talk about next.

2. With a partner, role-play a conversation between two people who have just met. Think about how these people might introduce themselves.

Pronunciation ACTIVITIES

Sentence Stress

In Chapter 1, you learned that English *words* have stressed and unstressed syllables. English *sentences* also have stressed and unstressed parts. English speakers stress words that are important to meaning—such as nouns, verbs, adjectives, adverbs, and question words. These are called *content words.*[1] They usually do not stress words that are important to grammar, such as articles, prepositions, conjunctions, helping verbs, and most pronouns. These are called *function words.*

Think about the stress in the following words and phrases. Compare the stress in the word with the stress in the phrase, and notice the similarities between the two.

Example:	ba	ba	BA	ba
	un	der	STAND	ing
	if	you	WANT	to

Example:	ba	BA	ba	ba
	im	POSS	i	ble
	I	LOOKED	at	him

[1] *This, that, these,* and *those, yours, mine, ours, theirs, myself, yourself, himself, herself, yourselves, ourselves,* and *themselves* are also content words.

TALKING POINT

Learning English sentence stress (rhythm) is usually the most important thing that a student can do to improve his or her accent. If rhythm is difficult for you, try tapping a pencil against the table to help you emphasize the content words. Try to shorten the function words by contracting them.

Predict Sentence Stress

Look at the following sentences from the conversation. Underline the content words that you expect to be stressed. Refer to the previous pronunciation box to see which words are content words.

1. I just started there this week.

2. We put in long days, but it's a great place to work.

3. I heard about that in the interview.

4. I've been wondering what there is to do around here.

5. Next Sunday we've planned a picnic at the park near work.

Practice Sentence Stress

As you listen to the following sentences from the conversation, underline the words that are stressed. Then, check to see whether the predictions that you made were correct.

1. I just started there this week.

2. We put in long days, but it's a great place to work.

3. I heard about that in the interview.

4. I've been wondering what there is to do around here.

5. Next Sunday we've planned a picnic at the park near work.

Listen to these sentences again, repeating each after the speaker. Focus on stressing the content words and not stressing the function words.

Practice Pronouncing Sentence Stress

With a partner, fill in the missing lines in the following dialog in any way
that you think makes sense. Underline the content words that you should
stress when saying the dialog. Take turns playing Jan and Ryan, and practice saying the sentences with the correct stress.

Jan: Hey! How are you?
Ryan: _____

Jan: Pretty good. My classes are really tough, though.
Ryan: _____

Jan: Well, I'm a science major, and I have to take math this term, so
there are lots of tests. I've had to cut down on my hours at work. Are
you still working in the dining hall?
Ryan: _____

Jan: Yeah, it's nice now, but I hear it's supposed to rain this weekend.
Ryan: _____

Jan: Where are you going now?
Ryan: _____

Jan: Well, I have to go to class. See you later.
Ryan: _____

Role-Playing

Role-play a conversation between two people who are making small talk.
You may use ideas from the dialog, but do not memorize or read it.
Practice using correct sentence stress while speaking spontaneously. To
check your pronunciation, perform the dialog on tape or for others in your
class.

TALK It Up!

Starting a Conversation and Keeping It Going

Conversing in English is a great way to improve your fluency and vocabulary, but some students of English find it difficult to start a conversation with people whom they do not know well. Other students discover that simply answering questions is not enough and that their conversations in English end too quickly for them to get much practice. Here are some tips and strategies to help you overcome these challenges.

Starting a Conversation

- Talk about something that you and this person have in common:
  "You're in Econ 151, aren't you?"
  "The bus is late today."

- Ask a question:
  "Have you read any books by that author?"

- Talk about current events, weather, or sports:
  "Did you see the game last weekend? Do you know what the final score was?"

Keeping a Conversation Going

- Listen carefully, and make eye contact with the speaker.
- Respond to the speaker so that he or she knows that you are listening. Nod your head or say, "uh-huh," "really?" "yeah," or some other phrase to show that you are listening.
- When you answer a question, ask a question in return. If you cannot think of a question, try to give an answer that has more detail than "yes" or "no."

Compare:
A: Have you read any other books by that author?
B: No.
  OR
A: Have you read any other books by that author?
B: No. My friend recommended this book. Have you read any of this author's books?

Brainstorm More Ideas

There are many more ways to start conversations and keep them going. After you read the previous list, work with others in your class to brainstorm at least three more ideas.

More ways to start a conversation:

_____

_____

_____

_____

More ways to keep a conversation going:

_____

_____

_____

_____

_____

Role-Playing

With a partner, role-play a conversation between two people who have just met. Think about how these people might introduce themselves. Before you start, answer the following questions with your partner.

1. How will you start the conversation? (Choose one.)

    ____ Talk about something that you have in common? _____

    ____ Ask a question? _____

    ____ Talk about current events? Weather? Sports?

    ____ Pay a compliment? _____

2. Plan a second question that you could ask about the topic that you chose in question 1.

    _____

3. During your conversation, be sure to
    • introduce yourself,
    • make eye contact,
    • show that you are listening, and
    • ask questions to keep the conversation going.

On Your Own

Introduce yourself to someone in your building or your school whom you would like to meet, or go to a student center or cafe and introduce yourself to someone there. Tell the class or a small group about your meeting.

Listening Three
Workplace Challenges

You will hear an industrial technician talk about her job. Remember to focus on hearing the content words to help you to understand main ideas.

Before You Listen

For the following questions, note your answers on the lines provided and then compare your answers with a partner's.

1. What kind of work do you think an industrial technician does?

    _____

2. What do you think that she will talk about?

    _____

3. How do you know when someone thinks that you are not doing a good job at work or school? What would you do if you suspected your boss or teacher was not happy with your work?

    _____

Listen for Main Ideas

 Listen to the industrial technician talk about her job, and then choose the correct answer to each of the following questions.

1. She works at a(n) _____ company.
    a. automobile   b. bicycle   c. industrial

2. She has _____ problems at work.
    a. many   b. some   c. few

3. She thinks she might be a good _____ .
    a. teacher   b. student   c. manager

Take Notes

 Listen carefully, and then write the answers to the questions in the following chart in note form. Compare your notes with a partner's. You may listen again if needed.

What does she do at work?	
What problems does she have on the job?	
How does she plan to solve her problems?	
What might she want to do in the future?	

After You Listen

Retelling the Story

Imagine that you are talking to a friend who says he is not happy with his job. Use the notes that you took in the chart to tell, in your own words, the industrial technician's story to your friend.

Solving Problems

The industrial technician talks about a problem that she is having at work. She has not gotten much of a raise since she began, and she thinks that her boss does not like her work. Try to help her to solve these problems by suggesting positive ways that she could use to bring up this subject with her boss.

Read the following list of ways that the industrial technician could start a conversation with her boss, and add an idea of your own to the list. Then rank these ways in order from most positive to least positive. Put a 1 next to the most positive, a 2 next to the second most positive, and so on.

____ I'd like to talk to you about my performance review. Do you have a few minutes?

____ Could you give me your opinion about my work on the bike frame project I've been working on?

____ You don't like my work, do you?

____ I'd like to know if you are pleased or disappointed with my work.

____ _____

Further Practice

Self-Evaluation

By now, you should be able to find some of your mistakes on your own and correct them. Return to the pronunciation and fluency test in the preface, and record the test again using the following paragraph and picture. Listen to your recording. What errors can you find? Re-record any words or phrases that you mispronounced, and try to correct your mistakes. Then, with your teacher's help, answer the following questions.

1. What has improved?

   _____

2. What will you work on next?

   _____

Record the results of your self-evaluation in the chart on page xviii.

Jack of All Trades

Some people call Sherman a "Jack of all trades." You see, he's had a great variety of jobs in his lifetime. In high school, he worked part-time as a photographer for a local newspaper. He also spent a summer working at an amusement park. He didn't really like these jobs, though. So when he finished high school, he took a job at a zoo. He spent eight hours a day taking people's money and helping them read their zoo maps. Usually he liked it, but sometimes it was boring. What did Sherman do? He quit and went back to school. He entered a community college to study forestry. To help pay college expenses, he worked nights in a toy factory and weekends painting sets in a theater. Soon, Sherman will graduate, so he's starting to look for employment again.

Small Talk

To practice small talk, have a "get to know you" party in class. You can do either of the following.

- Invite another class to visit your class, and then students can practice introducing themselves and meeting new people.
  OR
- Each student in your class can create a "new" identity and pretend to be that person at the "party." Think of a new name, profession or major, age, and personality for yourself. You may even change the country in which you were born. When you come to class, make a name tag for yourself and pin or tape it to your clothes. Practice making small talk with all of the "new" people that you meet at the party. You might want to write answers to the following questions about your new identity and carry them with you.

1. What is your new name?

2. What is your new major or profession?

3. From what city, town, or country does the new you come?

4. How long has the new you lived where you do now?

5. What other details about your new identity do you need to remember?

This is your chance to be anyone you want to be!

Class Project: Speaking to an Expert[2]

Find out if your school has a career center. If so, visit the center or invite a career counselor to talk to your class.

1. Before the counselor arrives, the class forms small groups. Each group brainstorms at least five questions to ask the counselor about (a) services that the center has for students, (b) employment opportunities during and after college studies, or (c) job-hunting skills.

   Write your group's questions on the following lines.

   _____

   _____

   _____

   _____

   _____

2. Each group in the class chooses two or three questions to report. From these collected questions, make a short list of about five questions. This list should be typed and given to the counselor before she or he arrives.

3. Take notes on the information that the counselor gives you. Ask any questions that you had that were not answered.

4. After the counselor's visit, compare notes with those of others in your group and add any information that is missing from your notes.

5. Use your notes to help you to talk about what you heard the counselor say. Practice until you can explain clearly and at a good speed, without reading from your notes. Then record your explanation on a tape. Give the tape to your teacher for feedback.

[2]If a career counselor is not available, ask a teacher or staff member at your school to talk about the training and the academic choices that led him or her to this occupation.

5

School Choices/ Life Opportunities

CHAPTER HIGHLIGHTS

Listening	Pronunciation	Speaking	Class Project
Listen for context and attitudes	/s/, /ʃ/, and /tʃ/	Make suggestions	Conduct a survey
Listen for details	Intonation	Participate in a group discussion	
Listen for main ideas			
Take notes			

Brainstorming

Help on Campus

The following directory tells where to get services on a college campus.

> ### Campus Directory
>
> Admissions Office . . . . Campus Center
> Bookstore. . . . . Campus Center
> Career Center . . . . Lee Hall
> Counseling and Advising . . . . Lee Hall
> Financial Aid. . . . . Administration Building
> Health and Wellness Center. . . . . Campus Center
> Learning Skills Center . . . . Campus Center
> Library. . . . . Cook Library
> Parking and Transportation Services . . . . Administration Building
> Recreation and Sports . . . . Brodie Gymnasium

Use this directory to answer the following questions.

1. Where can I find out about a loan to cover college tuition?

   _____

2. Where can I go on campus to get advice about my resume?

   _____

3. Where should I go to do research for one of my classes?

   _____

4. I am having trouble in some of my classes. Where can I get some help?

   _____

5. Which office can help me to figure out my general education requirements?

   _____

6. Which office can answer a question about student health insurance?

   _____

Discuss your answers with others in your class. Think of two more questions that students might have, and discuss with other classmates which offices might have the answers to them.

Listening One
Asking for Advice

Dr. Shaeffer is a professor of business administration. One day, Sang Won, a student in one of her classes, stops by to ask for help.

Before You Listen

What would you do if you were not satisfied with your grades or progress in a class? Choose three of the following possible actions that you might take to solve this problem. Mark your first choice 1, your second 2, and your third 3.

____ Study harder.

____ Drop the class.

____ Meet with the professor during her office hours.

____ Get a tutor.

____ Ask a friend for help.

____ Cheat on a test.

____ Go to the school's learning center.

____ Other: _____

Discuss your choices with others in your class. What are the advantages and disadvantages of each?

Listen for Context and Attitudes

 Listen to the conversation between Dr. Shaeffer and Sang Won, and then answer the following questions.

1. When and where do you think that this conversation took place?
    a.   at Dr. Shaeffer's office during her office hours
    b.   after class in the classroom
    c.   in the afternoon outside on campus

2. How does Sang Won feel about his grade at the start of the conversation?

   a.   relieved

   b.   concerned

   c.   satisfied

3. How does Sang Won feel about his grade at the end of the conversation?

   a.   relieved

   b.   concerned

   c.   satisfied

Listen for Details

 Listen to the conversation again. Then, in the following list, check each action that Dr. Shaeffer recommends.

_____ Study harder.

_____ Drop the class.

_____ Meet with her during her office hours.

_____ Get a tutor.

_____ Ask a friend for help.

_____ Cheat on a test.

_____ Go to the school's learning center.

____ Other: _____

After You Listen

Role-Playing

Role-play the conversation between Sang Won and Dr. Shaeffer in one or more of the following ways. Be prepared to present one of these role-plays for the class.

1. Sang Won is a hard-working, confident student, and Dr. Shaeffer wants to help him. He feels comfortable talking to Dr. Shaeffer because she has a reputation for giving good advice.

2. Sang Won does not seem to be trying in class. Dr. Shaeffer has given him lots of advice, but he never follows that advice.

3. Sang Won is nervous about seeing Dr. Shaeffer. Other students say that her classes are really difficult and that she is always angry and too busy to talk to students.

Pronunciation
ACTIVITIES

/s/ as in sing, /ʃ/ as in shop, and /tʃ/ as in change

Look at the following drawings of mouth positions. How are the mouth positions the same, and how are they different?

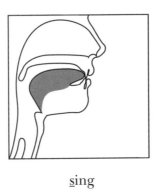
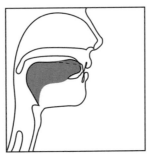
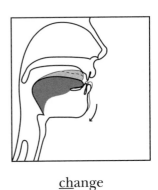

sing   shop   change

- For /s/, use the tip of the tongue to almost touch right behind the teeth. Push air through to make /s/.

  Examples: *sell, see, circle*

- To pronounce /ʃ/, use the front of your tongue to almost, but not quite, touch the *alveolar ridge* (the bump behind your teeth). Push air through to make /ʃ/.

  Examples: *shell, she, shoe*

- For /tʃ/, use the front of your tongue to touch the alveolar ridge. Stop the air, and then, as you let the air through, make /tʃ/.

  Examples: *change, check, cheese*

Practice /s/, /ʃ/, and /tʃ/ in Words

The following words from the conversation have one of the sounds /s/, /ʃ/, or /tʃ/. Underline the sound that you predict that you will hear. Then listen, and in the following list, circle the sound that you hear.

1. second	/s/ /ʃ/ /tʃ/		6. contributions	/s/ /ʃ/ /tʃ/
2. sure	/s/ /ʃ/ /tʃ/		7. change	/s/ /ʃ/ /tʃ/
3. challenging	/s/ /ʃ/ /tʃ/		8. center	/s/ /ʃ/ /tʃ/
4. chat	/s/ /ʃ/ /tʃ/		9. brush up	/s/ /ʃ/ /tʃ/
5. assignments	/s/ /ʃ/ /tʃ/		10. check	/s/ /ʃ/ /tʃ/

Listen to the words again, and repeat each after the speaker says it. Look at these words to see some ways that /s/, /ʃ/, and /tʃ/ can be spelled.

Practice /s/, /ʃ/, and /tʃ/ in Sentences

Listen to the following sentences from the conversation. Repeat each after the speaker. Practice saying /s/, /ʃ/, and /tʃ/ correctly.

1. You probably just need to change your study habits.

2. The short essay questions seem to be especially difficult for you.

3. They can help you brush up your writing and teach you some test-taking strategies.

4. And next term, you should consider taking an English class.

5. So you think I still have a chance to pass your class?

Practice Pronouncing /s/, /ʃ/, and /tʃ/

Student A: Check **one** phrase in each of the following pairs in the left-hand column. Do not tell Student B which you checked. Read it to Student B.

Student B: Listen to the phrase that Student A reads, and then check the appropriate ending from the right-hand column in the following list.

After you and your partner have completed all six items, compare your answers. Then, reverse roles and repeat the exercise.

1. _____ You should sign   _____ the check when you get to the bank.

   _____ You should shine   _____ your shoes before your job interview.

2. _____ Please show   _____ me those pictures of your family.

   _____ Please sew   _____ a button on my shirt.

3. _____ Are you using this sheet   _____ of paper?

   _____ Are you using this seat   _____ or can my friend sit here?

4. _____ I need to wash   _____ my clothes.

   _____ I need to watch   _____ a TV show for my history class.

5. _____ Did you chop   _____ down the tree?

   _____ Did you shop   _____ at the new store downtown yet?

6. _____ I saw her cheat   _____ on the test.

   _____ I saw her sheet   _____ of paper, but I didn't copy her answers.

Communicative Pronunciation Practice /s/, /ʃ/, and /tʃ/

With a partner, complete the following chart. Ask each other questions to find out what subject each person in the chart studies. Be sure to pronounce /s/, /ʃ/, and /tʃ/ correctly.

Student A: Look at this page.

Student B: Look at page 171 at the end of the book.

Example: A: What is Sue's major?

B: Sue's major is Chinese Literature. Who's studying English?

A: Charles is …

Sue: Chinese literature	Richard: Biotechnology	1. _____ : Communications	Roger: Sociology
2. _____ : English	3. _____ : Political science	Shelly: Early childhood education	Patricia: Special education
4. _____ : Engineering	Francheska: Psychology	5. _____ : French linguistics	Graciela: Sculpture
Latisha: Journalism	Virginia: Undecided	Mitch: 6. _____	Sharise: 7. _____

TALK It Up!

Making Suggestions

In the conversation between Dr. Shaeffer and Sang Won, Dr. Shaeffer offered suggestions about how Sang Won could improve his grades. To make suggestions, you can use *modals*, such as *should, might, could,* and *ought to* in phrases such as the following.

I think that you should …

You might want to …

Maybe you could …

You ought to try …

You might want to end your suggestion with some words of encouragement, such as the following.

Everything will work out.

Don't worry. Things will be OK.

If you … , you'll do fine.

Practice Making Suggestions

What must students do to be successful? Complete the following chart, using these steps to practice making suggestions to help students be successful.

1. In column one, list five concerns that a new student might have about being successful at school.

2. In column two, list suggestions about how to solve each concern.

Concerns That a Student Might Have	Suggestions About How to Solve This Concern
I might forget my assignments.	Write the assignments in a notebook.

Role-play a conversation between an experienced student and a student who is new to a school or a class. The new student should talk about the problems in column one, and the experienced student should use phrases from column two to make suggestions and offer encouragement.

Listening Two
Learning a Language

Kim has decided to take a French class, but she is nervous about studying a new language and about how it will affect her grade-point average (GPA). Since Barbara has studied Spanish for a long time, Kim asks her for advice.

Before You Listen

Some reasons why people decide to learn languages are listed next. Add a reason to the list, then mark the most important reason why you decided to study English. Discuss your reasons with others in your class.

_____ To learn about another culture

_____ To read literature in the language

_____ To get a better job

_____ _____

Listen to Understand Attitudes

 Listen to the conversation, and then answer the following questions.

1. How does Kim feel at the beginning of the conversation?

   _____

2. What is Barbara's attitude toward learning languages?

   _____

3. How does Kim feel at the end of the conversation?

   _____

Listen for Details

Kim tells Barbara her concerns about taking French, and Barbara gives Kim lots of advice and encouragement.

 Listen again, and in the following list, match the concern that Kim expresses to the encouragement that Barbara offers.

Kim's concerns:

____ She is not sure that she will do well in French.

____ She doesn't want to ruin her GPA.

____ She wonders if she should drop the course.

Barbara's encouragement:

a. Just be sure to get a lot of practice.

b. I took French. I did really well.

c. You might be opening up all kinds of possibilities.

After You Listen

What is your favorite subject to study? In a small group of classmates, share why you like to study this subject and what a student should do to learn it successfully.

Pronunciation ACTIVITIES

Intonation

One of the most important ways that speakers of English express their ideas and feelings is through intonation. *Intonation* is a change in the pitch of a word or sentence. That is, it is saying something with a higher or lower sound to give the word or sentence more meaning. Rising and falling intonation can have many different meanings, but one of its most common uses is to indicate questions and statements. In this section, you will practice hearing and pronouncing English intonation in questions and statements. In the following examples, arrows indicate rising and falling intonation.

- In an ordinary English statement, the intonation falls on the last content word in the sentence.

Examples: I'm going to the store.

She wants to speak to him.

- In a yes/no question, the intonation rises on the word about which the question is being asked. Usually, this is the last content word in the question.

Examples: Are you going to the store?

Does she want to speak to him?

- *wh* questions have a special intonation pattern. These questions start with the question words *who, what, when, where, why, which,* and *how.* The intonation rises and then falls on the word about which the question is being asked. Usually, this is the last content word in the question.

Examples: Where are you going?

Whom does she want to talk to?

Predict Rising and Falling Intonation

For each of the following sentences from the conversation, predict which intonation pattern that you will hear. Draw a rising arrow ⟋ or a falling arrow ⟍ to show rising or falling intonation.

1. Did you have a nice break?

2. How about you?

3. But I'm glad to be back.

4. How're your courses?

5. I took French one summer.

6. I'm a little worried.

7. If I don't do well, how will it look on my record?

8. Do you think I should drop the course?

9. Do you want her number?

10. Do you think she'd mind?

Practice Intonation

 Now listen to the sentences, and mark in the following list the intonation that you actually hear. After you listen, check to see whether your predictions in the previous exercise were correct. Then, listen to the sentences again, and repeat each after the speaker says it.

1. Did you have a nice break?

2. How about you?

3. But I'm glad to be back.

4. How are your courses?

5. I took French one summer.

6. I'm a little worried.

7. If I don't do well, how will it look on my record?

8. Do you think I should drop the course?

9. Do you want her number?

10. Do you think she'd mind?

TALKING POINT

Sometimes, in informal spoken English, people use intonation to indicate questions instead of using question word order or question words. In such questions, intonation is the only way that the listener knows that the sentence is a question.

Practice Pronouncing Intonation

Student A: Check **one** phrase in each of the following pairs in the left-hand column. Do not tell Student B which you checked. Read it to Student B.

Student B: Listen to the phrase that Student A reads, and then check the appropriate ending from the right-hand column in the following list.

After you and your partner have completed all six items, compare your answers. Then, reverse roles and repeat the exercise.

1. ____ We have to read 40 pages for homework?   ____ Yes, we do.
   ____ We have to read 40 pages for homework,   ____ so we had better get started.

2. ____ You paid the insurance fee,   ____ so you can use the health center for free.

   ____ You paid the insurance fee?   ____ No, I use my parents' insurance plan.

3. ____ He has already registered for classes,   ____ but I haven't registered yet.
   ____ He has already registered for classes?   ____ I thought we were supposed to register next week.

4. ____ We have class today?   ____ Of course not! It's Saturday.
   ____ We have class today,   ____ but tomorrow is a school holiday.

5. ____ They're taking an English class this term   ____ so that they can improve their writing skills.

   ____ They're taking an English class this term?   ____ I thought that they took it last term.

6. ____ Your roommate finished her essay?   ____ No, she's still working on it.
   ____ Your roommate finished her essay.   ____ Really? I'm glad she's finished.

Communicative Pronunciation Practice

Complete the following dialog with phrases or sentences. Use rising and
falling arrows to mark the correct intonation on the parts that you added.
Then, perform the dialog with a partner. Use these arrows to help you to
use the correct intonation.

This dialog takes place in the student bookstore:

A. Have you registered for next term's classes?

B. _____

A. Yeah, I did. It's going to be a difficult term. I have a full load.

B. _____

A. Two classes in my major, my math requirement, my foreign language

requirement, and human biology. Hey, you took human biology,

didn't you?

B. Yeah, I did. Last term.

A. _____

B. Not too bad. We had multiple choice tests and one short paper.

A. _____

B. I thought it was really interesting.

A. Have you decided what classes you'll take?

B. _____

A. _____

B. _____

A. _____

B. _____

TALK
It Up!

Participating in a Group Discussion

In many academic and professional situations, you will have to participate in group discussions. In fact, your grades at school or promotions at work might depend on how well you express your ideas and involve others in discussions. The following strategies can help you to become a better discussion participant.

- Prepare for the discussion by reading or thinking about the discussion topic.
- Make notes of your ideas so that you can refer to them during the discussion.
- Do not dominate the discussion! If you tend to talk a lot in discussions, plan some questions that you can ask other participants.
- Do not expect everyone to agree with you. Express your opinions freely, but do so politely by using phrases such as the following.

Agreeing:

> That sounds right to me too, because …
> Another example of that is …
> That's exactly how I feel.
> I couldn't have said it better myself. In fact, …
> I agree with you because …

Disagreeing:

> Let me give you an example of why that idea might not work so well.
> Are you forgetting about … ?
> If you look at it this way, you'll see that this idea doesn't always work.
> I disagree because …
> I don't agree with that at all because …!

Practice Participating in a Discussion

In some educational systems, students are required to study a second language at an early age. In other systems, students study second languages much later or maybe do not study them at all.

Discuss in a group the following two approaches to education. First, the group lists the advantages and disadvantages of each. Then, it decides which approach it thinks is the best.

Advantages   Disadvantages

Early Language Education

_____   _____
_____   _____
_____   _____
_____   _____

Later Language Education

_____   _____
_____   _____
_____   _____
_____   _____

Finally, discuss in the group whether you agree and disagree with its conclusions. Remember that your purpose is to share different reasons for your ideas and not to make everyone agree with you.

Listening Three
Being Bilingual—What an Advantage!

Speaking more than one language is a challenge. Being bilingual or trilingual also can be an advantage; it can lead to unexpected opportunities. Listen to this interview with two multilingual people. You might not understand every word that you hear, but you will understand more than you did in earlier chapters. Focus on what you do understand. You will have opportunities to discuss the information and listen again.

Before You Listen

Think about how you learned the languages that you know and the advantages that knowing them offers you. Then complete the following chart.

What languages do you know?	How did you learn them?	What advantages do they offer?

Listen for Main Ideas

 Listen to the interview, and then complete the first column of the following chart (What languages does this person know?).

	What languages does this person know?	How did this person learn these languages?	What advantages does knowing these languages offer?
First Speaker			
Second Speaker			

Take Notes

 Listen again and complete the second and third columns of the chart.

After You Listen

With a partner or on tape, retell, in your own words, the stories that you just heard. When working with a partner, one of you should tell the story of the first speaker, and the other should tell the story of the second speaker.

Further Practice

Class Project: Conducting a Survey

Do a survey to learn more about what people think of studying foreign languages. Follow these steps.

1. In a group of classmates, decide what group of people you will survey. For example, you might want to survey native speakers of English, other students, or teachers.

2. Decide on four or five survey questions. and write or type them on a piece of paper. Each group member should have a copy of the questions.

3. Each group member surveys five people. Before beginning, each should review the interviewing skills on page 7 in Chapter 1.

4. If an interviewee gives a very short answer, the interviewer should ask him or her to tell more. The interviewer might say, "Can you tell me more?" or "That's really interesting! What else can you tell me?"

5. Meet with your group to compare the results of your survey. Summarize the results by identifying similarities and differences in the answers and giving percentages of similar answers. You might want to make a table or graph to illustrate your results.

6. In a new group of people from different survey teams, present your summarized results.

6

Money Matters

CHAPTER HIGHLIGHTS

Listening	Pronunciation	Speaking	Class Project
Make predictions	Practice focal stress	Participate in a	Work with pie charts
Listen to details	/r/ and /l/	discussion	
Follow instructions		Use telephone	
Listen for specific		information systems	
information		Listen and respond	
Summarize main ideas			
Take notes			

Brainstorming

Managing Money

Answer the following questions in note form, and then discuss them with other classmates in a small group. Write your classmates' answers in the chart that follows the questions.

1. Do you manage your money differently from the way that you did five years ago? How have your methods of money management changed?

2. Do you prefer to do your banking in person at the bank, online, by telephone, or at an automated teller machine (ATM)? Why?

3. Do you have a credit card? If so, how often do you use it? What kind of purchases do you make with it?

	Your Answer	Classmate's Answer Name:	Classmate's Answer Name:
Question 1.			
Question 2.			
Question 3.			

Summarize the results of your discussion for others in your class, or record your summary on tape for homework.

Listening One
Credit Card or Debit Card? You Decide!

Kim doesn't buy on credit, but she needs a credit card for emergencies, so she goes to the bank to apply for one.

Before You Listen

Making Predictions

What words and phrases do you think that Kim will need to use at the bank? In the following list, put an X next to the words that you expect to hear. Compare your predictions with a partner, and discuss any differences in your choices.

____ credit card	____ application
____ debit card	____ checking account
____ credit check	____ interest rate
____ annual fee	____ bank statement
____ loan	____ budget

Listen to Check Your Predictions

As you listen to Kim's conversation at the bank, mark in the following list each word or phrase that you hear. Were your predictions correct?

____ credit card	____ application
____ debit card	____ checking account
____ credit check	____ interest rate
____ annual fee	____ bank statement
____ loan	____ budget

Listen for Details

Listen again. This time, listen for the details about the card that Kim wants to get. Then, answer the following questions.

1. What is the difference between a credit card and a debit card?

   _____

2. Does Kim want a credit card or a debit card? _____

3. What is the interest rate on the card? _____

4. What is the annual fee for the card? _____

5. What is the interest rate on the car loan that Kim's friend has? _____

Listen and Respond

Listen to the beginning of this conversation, and when the recording stops, finish the conversation with a partner. Your conversation may end differently from Kim's or in the same way. Be prepared to share your ending with the class.

After You Listen

Would a credit card, a debit card, or both be better for you? What are the advantages and disadvantages of each? Fill in the following chart. Compare your chart with a partner's.

Type of card	Advantages	Disadvantages
Credit card		
Debit card		

Pronunciation ACTIVITIES

Focal Stress in Sentences

English sentences have stressed words and unstressed words, just as words have stressed and unstressed syllables. In sentences, changes in stress can be used to change the meaning of a sentence or to focus on important information. Practice the following common conversation with a partner. Listen carefully to hear how you stress the words in the following sentences and phrases.

> A: Hi! How are you?
> B: I'm fine. How are you?
> A: I'm all right.

Usually, native speakers of American English would stress these sentences as follows.

> A: Hi! How are you?
> B: I'm fine. How are YOU?
> A: I'm all right.

Notice that the second *you* gets extra stress. This is because speaker B wants to emphasize that the question now is directed at speaker A. That is, there is a change in the focus of the conversation from speaker B to speaker A. This extra stress, which shows a change in focus, is called *focal stress*.

Practice Focal Stress in Sentences

In the conversation in this section, the bank representative uses focal stress to emphasize the difference between two things. Speakers also use focal stress when they want to emphasize new information or ask a question about a word that was just said.

 Listen to the conversation. Then, underline in the following sentences the words that get focal stress.

Kim:	I'd like to apply for a credit card.
Bank Representative:	A credit card or a debit card?
Kim:	What's the difference?
Bank Representative:	A credit card loans you the money, but you pay interest on the money you borrow.
Kim:	Hmm. What's the interest rate?

Listen again, and repeat each sentence after the speaker. Stress the words the way that the speakers do.

Practice Pronouncing Focal Stress

Mark the focal stress in the following conversations by underlining the stressed syllables. Then, practice reading the conversations, paying attention to the stress. The first one has been done for you.

Example: A: I'd like to open a <u>bank</u> account.
B: Do you want a savings account or a <u>check</u>ing account?
A: I guess I want a <u>check</u>ing account. Is there a minimum <u>bal</u>ance on the checking account?
B: Yes. Two hundred <u>doll</u>ars is the minimum balance.
A: And on the <u>sav</u>ings account?
B: <u>One</u> hundred dollars is the minimum.

A: What are you doing?

B: I'm looking at this bank statement.

A: Your bank statement?

B: No. My sister's bank statement.

A: Why are you looking at her bank statement?

B: I'm doing her banking while she's out of the country.

A: I always run out of money at the end of the month.

B: I thought you said that you had some extra money this month.

A: That was last month. This month I'm running short again.

B: You need to make a budget.

A: I have a budget. I just can't follow it.

A: Where are you going?

B: To the bank. I need a loan.

A: A loan? What kind of loan?

B: A car loan.

A: Are you buying a car?

B: I want to buy a car, but first I need a loan.

Communicative Pronunciation Practice

For more practice, write a short conversation about applying for a credit card or another kind of bank card. Mark the focal stress in the conversation by underlining the stressed syllables. Practice your conversation with a partner. Be prepared either to perform it in class or to record it on tape so that you can listen and check your own pronunciation.

TALK It Up!

Participating in a Discussion

Nowadays, people are carrying less cash and using credit cards and debit cards instead. Sometimes people refer to these cards as "plastic." Discuss in a group which method is better for paying for things: cash or plastic? Plan for this discussion by summarizing on the following lines what you have learned and what you know about these different methods of paying for things.

Advantages of Using Cash

_____

_____

_____

_____

_____

Disadvantages of Using Cash

_____

_____

_____

_____

_____

Advantages of Using Plastic

_____

_____

_____

_____

Disadvantages of Using Plastic

_____

_____

_____

_____

Discuss your ideas with your group's members, and explain which method of payment is most common, in your experience.

Listening Two
Banking by Phone

Many banks now let you complete bank transactions over the telephone. Banking is only one of the many services and information that you can get by using interactive telephone information systems.

Telephone Information Systems

When you call a telephone information system like those that many banks now have, you can get personalized information by pushing the buttons on a touch-tone telephone. The system's computer will ask for your identification number. After you enter this number by pressing buttons on the telephone keypad, the computer will give you a list of options from which to choose. This list is called a *menu.* Each time that you hear a menu of options, you then choose one option by pushing the correct number on the telephone keypad.

Information systems like these enable you to get information at any time without having to wait until a person is available to take your call. The system also enables you to listen as many times as you need so that you can be sure that you understand what is said. In this way, you do not feel that you are bothering people by asking them to repeat the same thing many times.

TALKING POINT

Calling a recorded telephone message can be a good way to practice listening to English because you can call back several times to check your understanding.

In this section, you will practice listening to information and choosing the correct numbers on a telephone keypad to complete a bank transaction.

Before You Listen

For each of the following bank transactions, match the method of money management that you prefer.

Transactions

____ Check the balance in your checking account.

____ Deposit money into your savings account.

____ Cash a check.

____ Apply for a loan.

____ Withdraw cash from your account.

____ Transfer money from checking to savings.

Money Management Techniques

  a. Visit the bank.

  b. Use the telephone.

  c. Use an ATM.

  d. Use a computer.

Explain your choices to others in your class.

Listening

Look at the following picture of a checkbook. Imagine that you forgot to write down the amount for check number 414. You could call your bank's Bank by Phone system to check the amount.

Listen to Follow Instructions

 Listen to the recording. Pause it when you hear each tone so that you can write down the number that you should push on your touch-tone telephone to find out the missing check amount.

1. Which number do you push to access your checking account? _____

2. Which number do you push to find out the amount of check number 414? _____

Listen for Specific Information

 Look again at the checkbook in the picture on page 111. Now listen to hear the missing check amount. Write that amount in the checkbook register.

Listen for Details

 Listen again, and mark in the following list two other bank transactions that you could make using this Bank by Phone system.

____ Make a loan payment.

____ Check your account balance.

____ Apply for a credit card.

____ Leave a message for the bank.

____ Transfer money from one account to another.

After You Listen

Answer the following questions, then share your answers with the class.

1. How easy or difficult do you think that this system is to use?

   _____

2. Would you use a Bank by Phone system? Why or why not? When might you use it?

   _____

3. What questions should you ask the bank about this system before you use it?

   _____

4. What other interactive telephone systems do you know about?

   _____

/r/ as in red and /l/ as in light

Many students of English have trouble pronouncing one or both of these sounds: /r/ and /l/. Some students confuse them. Other students make an /r/ sound that differs from the English /r/ sound. In this section, you will practice hearing and pronouncing these sounds. With your teacher and classmates, listen to see which of these sounds (if any) are difficult for you so that you can work on them.

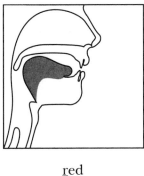
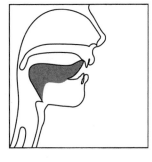

<u>r</u>ed   light

- For /r/, keep your tongue in the very middle of your mouth. It might help to keep the tip of your tongue up a little. Do not let the tip of your tongue touch any part of your mouth. Let the sides of your tongue touch your side teeth.

    Example: *red, right, read*

- To pronounce /l/, touch the alveolar ridge (the bump behind your teeth) with the tip of your tongue. To make the /l/ sound, you must let the air move around the sides of your tongue.[1]

    Example: *little, light, listen*

[1] When /l/ comes at the end of a word, the tongue is raised in the back of the mouth to touch the soft palate and the front to touch the alveolar ridge. This is sometimes called a "dark" /l/ and has a slightly different sound than the /l/ in the beginning and middle of words.

TALKING POINT

To help you pronounce /r/ and /l/, remember this touch/no touch rule.
- /r/: Tongue tip does not touch any part of your mouth.
- /l/: Tongue tip touches the ridge behind your teeth.

Practice /r/ and /l/ in Words

You will hear a list of words from the recording which have either an /r/ or an /l/ sound.

Write down the words that you hear.

1. _____   6. _____

2. _____   7. _____

3. _____   8. _____

4. _____   9. _____

5. _____   10. _____

Listen to the words again, and repeat each after the speaker. Be careful to pronounce the /r/ and /l/ sounds correctly.[2]

Practice /r/ and /l/ in Sentences

In the following sentences from the conversation in this section, circle the words that contain /r/ and /l/ sounds.

1. For savings accounts, press one.

2. To transfer to a service representative, press zero.

3. To return to the main menu, press star.

4. For the last three checks cleared, press three.

5. The balance is nine hundred seventy three dollars, eleven cents.

Then, listen to the conversation and repeat these sentences after the speaker to practice saying /r/ and /l/ correctly.

[2] Remember that /r/ can also be spelled *wr* as in *write*.

Practice Pronouncing /r/ and /l/

Student A: Check **one** question in each of the following pairs in column one. Do not tell Student B which question you checked. Read the question to Student B.

Student B: Listen to the question that Student A reads. Check the appropriate response in column two of the following list.

   After you have completed all six items, compare your answers. Then, reverse roles and repeat the exercise.

Student A   **Student B**

1. ____ Was that the long answer?   ____ No, it was the short one.
   ____ Was that the wrong answer?   ____ No, it was the right one.

2. ____ Is that the right bag?   ____ No, I left the right one at home.
   ____ Is that the light bag?   ____ Yes, the other one is heavier.

3. ____ Is she a good reader?   ____ Yes. She remembers what she reads, too.
   ____ Is she a good leader?   ____ Yes. People like to work with her.

4. ____ Did they see the clown?   ____ No, they didn't go to the circus.
   ____ Did they see the crown?   ____ Yes, it was on the king's head.

5. ____ Did you bring the supplies?   ____ Yes, we're all ready for the camping trip.
   ____ Did you bring the surprise?   ____ Yes, let's go to the party.

6. ____ Do you pray with your family?   ____ We pray every day.
   ____ Do you play with your family?   ____ Sometimes we play games together.

Communicative Pronunciation Practice

With a partner, complete the following chart.

Student A: Look at this page.

Student B: Look at page 171 at the end of the book.

Ask your partner questions about the bank cards in the chart: interest rate, annual fee, credit limit, and other features. Be careful to pronounce the /r/ and /l/ sounds correctly.

Example: A. What is the interest rate for the Passport Card?
              B. 11.3 %. What is the credit limit on the American Expression card?

	Passport Card	American Expression	LauralBank	
Type of Card		credit		
Credit Limit		$3,000		
Annual Fee		$30	no fee	
Interest Rate		19.9%	no interest	
Other Features		1% cash back each year	none	

On Your Own

To fill in the last column in the chart, call a bank, or read a credit card ad from a newspaper or that you received through the mail. Share the information that you learned about the card with a small group or the whole class.

TALK It Up!

Calling Telephone Information Systems

Banks are not the only businesses that use telephone information systems. Many other companies now use them, including credit card companies, telephone companies, airlines, bus companies, train companies, movie theaters, and government offices. These systems offer you great opportunities to practice listening.

Follow these steps to gather information using a telephone information system. You might need a touch-tone telephone to do this activity.

1. Find the number for a local or toll-free telephone information system. Write in the following line the name of the business or organization that has that system and its telephone number:

    _____

2. What kind of information can you get when you call this number?
    a.   a transportation schedule
    b.   information about a product or service
    c.   personal account information
    d.   information about entertainment
    e.   other:_____

3. Call the number, and then answer these questions.
    a.   When the telephone is answered, must you
         speak to a person?   Yes   No
         push a number on your telephone to make a choice?   Yes   No
         enter information about yourself, such as an
         account number?   Yes   No
            do nothing except listen to the information?   Yes   No

    b.   Write down one thing that you can learn by calling this telephone information system.

         _____

    c.   For whom might this telephone number be useful? Why?

         _____

    Describe to a small group the type of information or services available at this telephone number.

Listening Three
The Trouble with Credit Cards

Credit card companies often try to sign up new customers through mail advertisements and special gifts. Some people receive several credit card applications each week! You will hear an interview with two people who know about the kind of trouble that you can get into with credit cards.

Before You Listen

Read each of the following statements about credit cards, and mark whether you think that the statement is true or false. Then write the reason for your choice.

1. Credit cards can be helpful when you need money in an emergency.

    True   False

    Why? _____

2. Credit cards fees and interest are very expensive.   True   False

    Why? _____

3. It is safer to carry credit cards in your wallet than it is to carry cash.

    True   False

    Why? _____

4. Everyone should have at least one credit card.   True   False

    Why? _____

Listen to Summarize Main Ideas

Listen to the interview. Then, mark in the following list the sentence that best summarizes the problem that these students have had with credit cards.

_____ They lost their credit cards, and someone used them to buy things illegally.

_____ They spent more money with credit cards than they could afford to repay.

_____ They were not able to get credit cards because they have bad credit.

_____ Their parents will not allow them to use credit cards.

Take Notes

Listen again, and then complete the following chart. Some spaces may be left blank if the speakers do not give information about the question.

	First Person	Second Person
What was the credit limit on the cards?		
When did this person know he or she was in trouble with the cards?		
How did he or she solve the problem?		
How did this person pay off the debt?		
What did he or she do with the cards?		
Does he or she still owe money?		

Vocabulary from Context

The people in the interview use some credit card terms and some idiomatic phrases as they describe their problems with credit cards. In the following list, choose the correct meaning of each of the terms and phrases. Listen again if needed.

to max out:

    a.   to use a credit card for all of your shopping

    b.   to lose a credit card

    c.   to spend the total amount of your credit limit

payment plan:

    a.   a bill from the credit card company

    b.   a budget

    c.   a schedule of payments for a debt

I paid over $400 in very real money:

    a.   The interest cost over $400, which was a real expense.

    b.   The credit card company required me to pay for the interest in cash.

    c.   I couldn't borrow the money from my parents.

full balance:

    a.   your credit limit

    b.   all of the money that is due

    c.   only the money that you are able to pay

Check your guesses with a partner, then with your class.

After You Listen

With a partner, use your notes to review the problem that the two people in the interview had with credit cards and how they solved these problems. One of you should describe the most important parts of the first person's story, and the other should describe the most important parts of the second person's story.

Further Practice

Self-Evaluation

Go back to the pronunciation and fluency test record in the preface and test yourself again using the following picture and paragraph. Listen to your recording. What errors can you find? If it is still difficult for you to hear your own mistakes, ask a classmate or your teacher to listen with you. Re-record any words or phrases that you mispronounced, and try to correct your mistakes. Then answer the following questions.

1. What has improved? _____

2. What will you work on next? _____

Record the results of your self-evaluation in the chart on page xviii in the preface.

A Cashless Society

Have you noticed that the way people use money is changing? Some experts have suggested that we are becoming a "cashless" society. People today often carry twenty dollars or less in their wallets, but have five or six plastic cards: credit cards and debit cards. They use these cards to buy things or withdraw money from the bank. Not many years ago, many people rushed to the bank on Fridays. Why did they do that? They wanted to cash their paychecks so that they would have cash on hand for the weekend. Now our paychecks are often automatically deposited into our checking accounts, and we know that we can get money easily from a machine 24 hours a day. It could soon become possible to avoid going to the bank altogether!

Class Project: Work with Pie Charts

People often use charts and graphs to show a picture of how money is spent. Look at the following pie chart, which shows how one student spends her money each month. Then use the chart to answer the questions that follow.

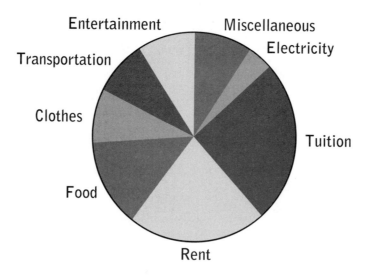

1. What is this student's biggest expense?

2. What kind of expenses might be in the miscellaneous category?

3. If this student wanted to save money, where might she spend less money?

Make a pie chart to present to a group of your classmates.

1. Choose a topic for your pie chart. A pie chart shows percentages, so you might use a pie chart to show your actual (or ideal) budget. Here are other possible topics.

   - What percentage of a group of people prefer to do their banking online, in the bank, at ATM machines, and by telephone?

   - What percentage of your purchases are paid for by check, by cash, by credit card, by debit card, and by automatic bank transfer?

   - How do you typically spend the 24 hours in your day?

2. If your pie chart will show a budget, complete the following table. If you have chosen a different topic, make a similar chart showing the items that will be in each section of your pie chart.

Percentage Spent

housing   _____

transportation   _____

food   _____

medicine/insurance   _____

entertainment   _____

telephone   _____

electric/gas   _____

savings   _____

miscellaneous   _____

other: _____   _____

3. Use the previous percentages to fill in the following pie chart.

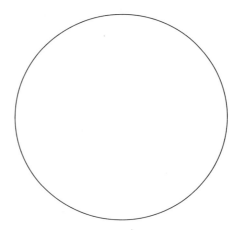

4. Give the chart a title.

5. Describe your pie chart to a small group or on tape. Review the tips for making presentations in Chapter 2 and use the following outline.

    I.   Introduce the chart, and explain the title.

    II.   List the categories represented in your chart.

    III. Point out the most interesting or important percentages represented.

    IV. Explain any trends in your spending or other conclusions that you can draw from this pie chart.

    V.   Determine the average spending habits for your group.

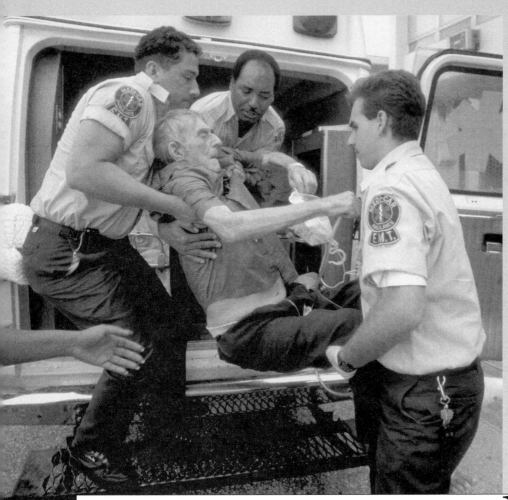

7

Help!

CHAPTER HIGHLIGHTS

Listening	Pronunciation	Speaking	Class Project
Get the gist	/θ/ and /ð/	Talk with an expert	Give travel advice
Listen for details	Linking	Use toll-free information numbers	
Listen for supporting information		Listen and respond	
Take notes			

Brainstorming

Everyone needs help sometimes. Perhaps you will never need emergency help, but it is always good to know what to do, just in case. In this chapter, you will find out about the many different kinds of help that people can get.

Discussion Questions

With a small group, discuss the questions from the following list that your teacher assigns to your group. Note your group's answers to the questions.

1. What telephone numbers do you know that you can call if you need emergency help? Have you ever had to call any of these numbers? How was your problem solved?

2. What other situations have you been in when you needed help? How did you feel? What kind of help did you need? How did you get it?

3. Tell the group about a time when you helped someone. Whom did you help? How did you help that person?

4. For what kind of help might you ask
   a.   a relative?
   b.   your best friend?
   c.   your teacher?

5. Who would you ask for help if you
   a.   needed help in a department store?
   b.   needed someone to help you to buy a used car?
   c.   were lost in an airport?

6. What would you do if someone were panicking? How would you calm that person?

Summarize your discussion for a new group or on tape for homework.

Listening One
An Emergency!

Dave and Alexander are studying together at Alexander's apartment one evening when the smoke alarm goes off.

Before You Listen

If you were in the situation described in the following pictures, what would you do? Share at least three suggestions with others in your class.

A

B

Listen to Get the Gist

Listen to the recording, and decide which of the pictures best illustrates the situation described in the recording. Circle your answer.

Listen for Details

Listen again to answer the following questions.

1. Why shouldn't Alexander put water on the fire? _____

2. How should he try to stop the fire? _____

3. What does Dave tell Alexander to do so that he won't breathe the
   smoke from the fire? _____

4. Was the person at the fire department angry that Dave called even
   though Dave and Alexander put the fire out? _____

5. Why do you think that the fire department is still coming to
   Alexander's apartment? _____

Listen and Respond

Listen again, and this time, stop the tape each time that you hear a pause.
Say the words that you think the person at the fire department might be
saying.

After You Listen

What do you already know about safety during emergencies and disasters?
    With a small group, list at least five safety tips for one of the following
situations. Remember to include tips about being prepared for and dealing
with the situation.

A fire in a building

An earthquake

A hurricane or other severe storm

A car accident

A fight

Other: _____

Pronunciation ACTIVITIES

/θ/ as in thing and /ð/ as in that

You make the *th* sounds by putting your tongue between your teeth and either blowing air through the space between your upper teeth and your tongue or blowing air around your tongue. English has two *th* sounds:

- The voiceless sound, /θ/, which begins such words as *think, thank,* and *thing*
- The voiced sound, /ð/, which begins such words as *this, that, these,* and *those*

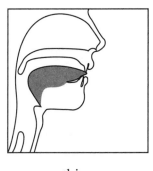   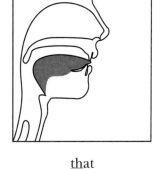

thing   that

TALKING POINT

Use a mirror to look at your mouth as you practice these two sounds. As you say /θ/ and /ð/, you should see the tip of your tongue between your teeth.

Practice /θ/ and /ð/ Words

You will hear a list of words from the conversation that have either a /θ/ or an /ð/ sound. Write down the words that you hear.

1. _____   6. _____

2. _____   7. _____

3. _____   8. _____

4. _____   9. _____

5. _____   10. _____

Listen to these words again, and repeat each after the speaker says it. Be careful to pronounce the /θ/ and /ð/ sounds correctly.

Practice /θ/ and /ð/ in Sentences

Listen to the following sentences from the conversation in this section and repeat after the speaker. Practice saying /θ/ and /ð/ correctly.

1. Try not to breathe the smoke.
2. I think it's getting better.
3. Everything seems to be under control again.
4. Sorry to bother you.
5. Were they angry that we called?

Practice Pronouncing /θ/ and /ð/

With a partner, take turns being Student A and Student B.

Student A: Check **one** question in each of the following pairs. Do not tell Student B which question you checked. Read it to Student B.

Student B: Listen to the question that Student A reads. Check the appropriate response from column two of the following list.

After you have completed all seven items, compare your answers. Then, reverse roles and repeat the exercise.

1. ____ Did you find a free pass ____ to the movies?
   ____ Did you find a free path ____ where we can ride our bikes?

2. ____ "He has a big mouth" ____ means he talks too much.
   ____ He has a big mouse ____ that he keeps as a pet.

3. ____ It was closing ____ so we didn't go into the restaurant.
   ____ It was clothing ____ that we wanted to buy at the store.

4. ____ Did you say "day" ____ or "night"?
   ____ Did you say they ____ are coming or not?

5. ____ There are three houses ____ and three cars in the picture.
   ____ There are tree houses ____ in the park where the children play.

6. ____ Is that the roof ____ of your house?
   ____ Is that the Ruth ____ you want me to meet?

7. ____ They gave free tickets ____ to everyone at the store.
   ____ They gave three tickets ____ to three lucky people.

Communicative Pronunciation Practice:
Giving Directions

If you ever call an emergency service such as the fire department, the hospital, or the police, you will probably need to give directions to your house.

Practice pronouncing the /θ/ and /ð/ sounds in the street names on the following map. Then, give directions to a partner that begin at the star that is in the center of the map and end at one of the points A, B, C, D, or E. Do not tell your partner which point you chose. Your partner should follow your directions to learn which you chose. Be sure to pronounce /θ/ and /ð/ correctly.

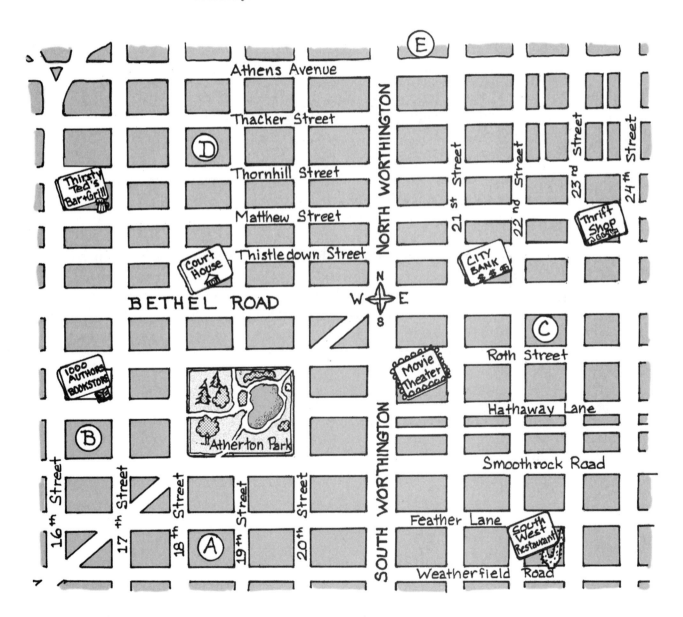

On Your Own

List several "th" words that you use often. Practice saying them correctly each day.

_____

_____

_____

TALK It Up!

Talk with an Expert

One of the best ways to learn more about a subject is to talk to an expert on the subject. You might find it intimidating to talk to someone who knows much more about a subject that you do. However, you can make this easier by preparing for your meeting with an expert, just as you would for a discussion or an interview.

To make your visit with an expert valuable for both of you, remember the following tips.

- Learn something about the subject that you will talk about ahead of time by reading or talking to others about it.
- Plan the questions that you will ask. You might want to give these questions to the expert ahead of time.
- If the expert says something that you don't understand, let him or her know right away. If you don't ask for an explanation early, the expert will assume that you understand and might then talk about things that are even more complicated.
- Remember the "Tips for Keeping a Conversation Going" on page 78 in Chapter 4. Use these tips to avoid awkward silences in your talk with the expert.
- At the end of your talk, thank the expert for his or her time.

TALKING POINT

Talking with an expert is excellent practice for academics and business, as it is similar to attending an academic class or a formal business meeting.

Ask someone from the fire department to visit your class to talk about fire safety.[1] Follow these steps.

1. Before the firefighter arrives, brainstorm with others in your class questions that you would like to ask him or her.

2. Each group in the class will choose two or three questions to add to the class's question list. This list should be typed and given to the firefighter before his or her visit.

3. Take notes on the information that the firefighter gives you during the visit. Ask any questions that you had that were not answered during the firefighter's presentation.

4. After the firefighter's visit, return to your group. Compare your notes to those of others in your class, and add any information that is missing from your notes.

5. In a small group or on tape, use your notes to help you to summarize the information that you received.

Your class also might want to sign and send a thank-you card to the firefighter.

---

[1] If it is not possible to invite a firefighter to visit, the class could call or write the fire department to request fire safety brochures or could visit fire safety sites on the Internet. The class can use information from these sources to find answers to their questions and to discuss what they discover.

Listening Two
The Missing Wallet

Viki is at a club with some friends. She leaves her wallet on a chair near the pool table while she plays. When she looks around, it is gone.

Before You Listen

In addition to money, a wallet usually contains bank cards, personal identification, and other important information. It is important to protect this information.

If your wallet is lost or stolen, what can you do to protect yourself and your money? Add at least three ideas to the following list.

1. *Cancel your credit card.* _____

2. _____

3. _____

4. _____

Listen for Supporting Information

Listen to Viki as she calls the police about her lost wallet. Then, in the following list, circle your opinion about what happened and write a reason or fact that supports your opinion.

1. Viki could have protected her wallet better   True   False

   because_____

2. Viki will get her wallet back   True   False

   because _____

3. The thief took a long time to plan this crime   True   False

   because _____

Listen for Details

Listen again to Viki's conversation with the police officer. Use her answers to complete the following Theft Report form.

Theft Report

Victim's name: _____

Victim's address: _____

Victim's telephone number: _____

Names of witnesses: _____

Where the theft occurred: _____

When the theft occurred: _____

Detailed description of stolen item(s): _____

_____

_____

Listen and Respond

Listen to the beginning of this conversation. When the recording stops, finish the conversation with a partner. Your ending may differ from Viki and Officer DeVeau's or be the same. Be prepared to share your ending with the class.

After You Listen

With a small group, discuss the following questions.

1. What should Viki have done to prevent this situation?

2. Viki called the police about a theft. What other kinds of help can you get from the police?

3. There is a saying in English: "An ounce of prevention is worth a pound of cure." This means that it is better to prevent a problem rather than to try to solve it. Is this saying true about Viki's problem? In what other situations is it true? Is this saying ever not true?

Pronunciation ACTIVITIES

Linking

When native speakers of American English talk, some of the words that they say might seem to "run together." In other words, you might find it difficult to hear where one word ends and the next begins. This is because in certain circumstances, words are *linked* together. Here are two examples of linking.

1. Consonant linking occurs when one word ends in the same consonant sound that the next word starts with. For example, in the phrase police station, the word police ends in the /s/ sound and the word station begins with /s/. Native speakers of American English will usually pronounce /s/ only one time: poli*ce s*tation. The following sentence has two words linked by consonants.

   Example: I fee*l l*ike reading a lot, so I'll ge*t t*wo books at the library.
                  /fiylayk/   /gɛtu/

2. *Consonant/vowel linking* occurs when a word that ends in a consonant sound comes before a word that begins with a vowel sound. This kind of linking is very common in American English, especially with some function words, such as *is, are, and, on,* and *at.* The following sentence has several examples of consonant/vowel linking.

   Example: I bough*t a* boo*k and a* magaz*ine at* the sto*re on* the corner.
                  /bɔtə/   /bʊkənə/   /mægəzinət/   /stɔrɑn/

Predict Consonant Linking

In the following sentences and phrases from Viki's conversation with the police, underline the words that are linked by consonant sounds. Remember to think about the sounds in the words and not just their spellings.

1. At Tempo, the club on Ninth Ave.
2. I'm there right now.
3. How long ago was it taken?
4. Maybe a little less.
5. It's red leather with three gold buttons on the edge.

Practice Consonant Linking

Now listen to these sentences and phrases. Try to hear the linkings, and then mark them in the sentences and phrases. Check your work here with your predictions in the previous section.

1. At Tempo, the club on Ninth Ave.
2. I'm there right now.
3. How long ago was it taken?
4. Maybe a little less.
5. It's red leather with three gold buttons on the edge.

Listen to the phrases again, and repeat each after the speaker. Make sure that you pronounce linked consonants as one consonant sound.

Predict Consonant/Vowel Linking

In the following sentences from the conversation, predict which words will have linked consonants and vowels and underline those words. Remember to consider the sounds in the words and not just their spellings.

1. I left it on a chair with some other things.
2. And I just looked away for a few minutes.
3. There're a lot of people here.
4. Inside there're pictures of family, friends.
5. Call us if you think of anything else.

Practice Consonant/Vowel Linking

Now listen to the sentences, and mark the consonant/vowel linking that you hear. Check your work here with your predictions in the previous section.

1. I left it on a chair with some other things.
2. And I just looked away for a few minutes.
3. There're a lot of people here.
4. Inside there're pictures of family, friends.
5. Call us if you think of anything else.

Listen to these sentences again, and repeat each after the speaker. Be sure to link the consonant and vowel in the linked words.

Practice Pronouncing Linking

Here are some short poems that parents often read to their children. In the first poem, the linking is marked for you. For the others, mark the linked words and then read the poems to practice linking. Ask a partner to listen to help you find out whether your linking is correct.

1. Star light, star bright,
   First star I see tonight,
   I wish I may, I wish I might,
   Have the wish I wish tonight.

2. There was an old woman
   Who lived in a shoe.
   She had so many children
   She didn't know what to do.

3. Mary had a little lamb.
   Its fleece was white as snow.
   And everywhere that Mary went,
   The lamb was sure to go.

On Your Own

Find a paragraph, poem, or song that you like. Mark the linkings, and then read your paragraph, poem, or song on tape. Listen to the tape yourself, or ask your teacher or a classmate to check the linking that you marked and your pronunciation.

TALK It Up!

Using Toll-Free Information Numbers to Get Help and Information

Many companies and organizations offer free information and help by way of toll-free numbers. Calling these numbers is a great way for you to get information and help on many different topics. In Canada and the United States, any number that begins with 1-800, 1-888, 1-866, or 1-877 is a toll-free number, meaning that you can call the number at no charge. You can often get tourist information, health information, or product information from companies by calling their toll-free numbers.

Each toll-free number works a little differently. At some numbers, you will speak to someone in person and at others, you will listen to recordings. Some organizations will send you information in the mail, and others will answer your questions over the telephone.

If you speak to someone in person, here are some tips to help you to request information.

- Introduce yourself, and then state the topic about which you need information. You could say:

    "I have a question about ____."

    "I'm calling to ask about ____."

    "Can you tell me more about ____?"

- Plan for the call as you would plan to speak to an expert. Make a note of your questions ahead of time.
- If your question is not answered by the person at the number that you called, ask that person about other sources of information. You could say:

    "Do you know where I could find out more about this?"

    "Is there any other organization that might be able to answer my question?"

- At the end of your call, thank the person for helping you.

1. Find a toll-free telephone number on a subject of interest to you, and write it here:

   _____

2. In a group, think of three questions that you think you could learn the answers to by calling this number. Then each of you should choose one question to ask when you call.

   _____

   _____

   _____

3. Call the telephone number, and ask your question. If you have trouble understanding the person who answers the telephone, ask the person to speak slowly and spell words that you don't know. You do not need to be nervous about calling. These people work at these numbers because they want to help people.

4. Take notes so that you will remember the answer to your question. If the person you are talking to gives you a local telephone number to call for more information, write down the number so that you can give it to your classmates.

   _____

   _____

   _____

   _____

   _____

   _____

5. Use your notes to report to your classmates on what you learned.

Toll-Free Information Numbers

To find toll-free numbers, check out the Internet toll-free directory at *www.inter800.com* or call 1-800-555-1212. You can also find toll-free numbers in magazine advertisements, on television, and on Internet Web pages. Here are some toll-free numbers that you might find useful.

Federal Information Center   **1-800-688-9889**

At this number, you will hear recordings about laws and programs sponsored by the U.S. government.

Jobs Network   **1-877-US-2-JOBS**[1]

Call this number to talk to a Jobs Network specialist and to ask about how to look for a job.

National Health Information Center   **1-800-336-4797**

At this number, you can get telephone numbers and addresses for health organizations that can give you information on any health topic.

Center for Food Safety and Nutrition   **1-888-723-3366**

At this number, you can listen to recorded messages about food safety, cosmetics, nutrition, seafood, and other topics. During the Center's business hours, you also can talk to a live person.

**U.S. Department of Agriculture Meat
and Poultry Hotline**   **1-800-535-4555**

By calling this number, you can ask a specialist about food safety or listen to messages about frequently asked food safety questions.

Prevent Child Abuse America   **1-800-556-2722**

The recording at this number will ask you for mailing information so that you can receive information from this organization in the mail.

Department of Transportation Auto Safety Hotline   **1-800-424-9393**

The recording at this number gives information about automobile and automobile equipment safety. You may speak to a representative or listen to the recordings.

[1] To call these numbers, use the letters on your telephone's keypad.

Listening Three
Bike Trip Check List

You will hear a student tell a story about a trip that she took across North America with two friends. The student also will give advice to other people who want to travel in a foreign country on bike. Remember, some words are linked together when a native speaker of English is speaking naturally so you may need to listen carefully.

Before You Listen

Before you go on a long trip, what kind of help do you need?

List three sources of information that you could turn to for help. A source of information can be, for example, a person, a place, a book, or an organization. Then write one question that you could ask for each source.

Source   Question That You Could Ask

1. _____   _____

                                                          _____

2. _____   _____

                                                          _____

3. _____   _____

                                                          _____

Take Notes

 Listen to the story to hear the three sources of information that the cyclist collected before taking her trip. Write these sources in the first column of the following chart.

Source of Information	Information You Can Get There

Take Notes

Listen again, and in the second column of the chart, note the kind of information available from each source.

After You Listen

With a partner or on tape, summarize the cyclist's story. Then call one of the sources of information that you talked about in the previous listening sections. Ask one question about a trip that you would like to take. Report to your classmates on your question and the answer that you received.

Further Practice

Class Project: Give Travel Advice

As group, think of a place that you all know well. Help someone who will travel to this place by giving them the information that they will need to have a good trip. Follow these steps.

1. Write the name of the place:_____

2. Write suggestions for the traveler about
   a. traveling in this place: _____
   b. the food in this place: _____
   c. safety tips: _____

3. Note three sources that a traveler could use to get more information about traveling in this place.
   a. _____
   b. _____
   c. _____

4. Plan and give a short presentation about traveling in the place that you chose. Follow this outline, and refer back to the presentation tips and feedback chart in Chapter 2.
   I.   Introduction: Tell listeners about the place about which you will talk. Describe the place and why a traveler would go there.
   II. Give your suggestions for traveling in this place.
   III. Give your suggestions for eating in this place.
   IV. Talk about your suggestions for staying safe in this place.
   V.   Discuss where a traveler could get information about this place.

Watching Television Shows Critically

TV shows about police officers fighting crime are very common. These feature some of the things that police officers do on the job, but usually they are not completely realistic. It is important to learn to be a critical viewer of television programs so that you can learn from television but not be fooled by it.

1. Watch a program about police officers, and fill in the following information.

   Name of the show: _____

   Channel: _____

   What the police officers on the show did: _____

   What you think some aspects are of a police officer's job that were not shown on the program: _____

   Words and phrases that you learned from the show:

   _____

2. Summarize to a group of classmates the plot of the show that you watched. Discuss your answers to the questions in number 1.

3. With a group, list things that you all saw in the shows that you believe are probably true. List other things that you saw that you believe are probably untrue.

8

Shopping

Listening	Pronunciation	Speaking	Class Project
Listen for purpose	Consonant clusters	Compare and contrast	Create a radio
Listen to numbers	/b/, /p/, and /f/	Use formal	program
Listen for main ideas		language	
Listen for details			
Take notes			

Brainstorming

Consumer Decisions

Whenever you shop, you make choices about the kind of store that you visit, how much money that you spend, and the companies whose products you support. In a small group or with a partner, talk about the choices that you make when you shop. Use the following chart to guide your discussion.

Questions	Name	Name	Name
Where do you like to shop? Why?			
What are your favorite things to buy?			
What is important to you when you shop? Cost? Quality?			

Listening One
Checking Out

Victor works as a cashier at a grocery store. On a typical day at his job, he has many conversations like the ones you will hear in this listening.

Before You Listen

Match each sentence on the left with the reason for talking to a cashier on the right.

1. _____ Could you tell me which aisle the soap is in?

2. _____ Can you change a ten?

3. _____ What's the total?

4. _____ Could you tell me how much this costs?

5. _____ I would like to return this.

6. _____ I think my cashier made a mistake.

a. Check the price of an item.

b. Pay for groceries.

c. Get change.

d. Get a refund.

e. Return an unwanted product.

f. Ask where an item is located.

Listen for Purpose

Listen to the conversations to find out why each person talks to Victor. Complete each of the following sentences with one of these phrases.

to check the price of an item

to pay for his/her groceries

to get change

to get a refund of his/her money

to return an unwanted product

to ask where an item is located

1. The first customer talks to Victor _____.

2. The second customer wants _____.

3. The third customer asks Victor _____.

4. The first customer returns because he/she needs _____.

Listen to Numbers

Listen to the four conversations to hear the answers to the following questions, and then fill in the blanks.

1. For how much money does the first customer write a check? _____

2. How much money does the second customer give Victor? _____

3. What is the sale price of the item that the second customer wants to buy? _____

4. What is the regular price of that item? _____

5. How much money does Victor give to the last customer? _____

After You Listen

Imagine that Victor works in a clothing store instead of a grocery store. What conversations might happen there?

Role-play with a partner several conversations that might occur between a salesperson and a customer in a clothing store.

Pronunciation ACTIVITIES

Consonant Clusters

English words often contain two or more consonants that are pronounced together because there is no vowel between them. Two, three, or four consonants that are pronounced together are called a *consonant cluster*. In the following words, the consonant clusters are underlined.

Examples:
<u>sw</u>im	/swɪm/
<u>str</u>eet	/striyt/
<u>tr</u>en<u>ch</u>	/trɛntʃ/
<u>pr</u>oblem	/prabləm/
<u>qu</u>iet	/kwayət/

If your language does not have consonant clusters, you might find clusters difficult to pronounce at first. /s/, /l/, /r/, and /w/ are often found in consonant clusters. Here are some hints for pronouncing these sounds in clusters.

- You will hear /s/ in many clusters because it slides into other sounds easily for native speakers of English. Be careful not to make two common mistakes when pronouncing clusters that have /s/.
  Do not add a vowel before the /s/.

  Example: *store* is pronounced /stɔr/ not /ɛstɔr/.

  Do not add a vowel between the /s/ and the other sound.

  Example: *store* is pronounced /stɔr/ not /sɛtɔr/.

- When you pronounce /l/, your tongue should touch the alveolar bump in the same place that it does for /t/, /d/, /s/, /z/, and /n/. Be sure that your tongue moves to touch this spot after you pronounce the consonant before it.

  Example: *pleasure* is pronounced /plɛʒər/.

- Don't let /r/ disappear from the cluster. Your tongue should move to the middle of your mouth to make this sound.

  Example: *true* is pronounced /truw/.

- Remember to suck in your cheeks as you pull your tongue away from the /t/ position.
- Make /w/ by rounding your lips. To help you to pronounce clusters that have a /w/, round your lips before you begin the consonant cluster.

  Examples: *twenty* is pronounced /twɛntiy/. *quarters* is pronounced /kwɔrtərz/. Round your lips when you say the /t/ and /k/ sounds. Notice that words that include *qu* are usually pronounced /kw/.

Practice Consonant Clusters in Words

Each of the following words from the conversation has one or more consonant clusters. When you hear the word, circle the consonant cluster(s).

1. driver's   6. special

2. excuse   7. true

3. twenty   8. problem

4. quarters   9. mistake

5. great   10. pleasure

Listen to the words again. Repeat each after the speaker says it to practice pronouncing consonant clusters.

TALKING POINT

Learn to pronounce a consonant cluster by first saying a word with only one of the sounds in the cluster. Then add sounds until you can say the cluster correctly.

Examples: rice → price
            rate → great
            sick → six → sixty
            mar → mark → marked

Practice Consonant Clusters in Sentences

Listen to the following sentences from the conversation, and repeat each after the speaker says it. Practice saying the consonant clusters correctly.

1. The shelf tag says it's on special incredibly cheap. I want to see if it's true.

2. Marked down from five dollars. That's a fifty percent discount.

3. That's a great price. Thanks!

4. I checked my receipt, and I was charged twice for this kitchen cleaner.

5. The scanner made the mistake, so you get them both for free.

Practice Pronouncing Consonant Clusters

With a partner or in a small group, practice pronouncing the following words. One student is the speaker, and the others are spellers.

Speaker: Mark one word from each group of words, and then pronounce the word.

Spellers: Spell the word that you hear.

Once the speaker has completed the list, change roles and repeat the exercise.

1. ____ glass   ____ grass   ____ gas
2. ____ quick   ____ kick   ____ click
3. ____ sport   ____ support   ____ sort
4. ____ parade   ____ prayed   ____ paid
5. ____ below   ____ blow   ____ bow (with /ow/ sound)
6. ____ asleep   ____ sleep   ____ seep
7. ____ address   ____ dress   ____ duress
8. ____ brand   ____ band   ____ bland
9. ____ world   ____ weld   ____ word
10. ____ tuck   ____ struck   ____ truck   ____ stuck

On Your Own

List six words that you use every day that have consonant clusters that are difficult for you to say. Practice these words every day until you can use them easily at any time.

_____   _____

_____   _____

_____   _____

Communicative Pronunciation Practice

Work in a small group to buy presents for each of the following people. For each person, decide, as a group, how much to spend, what to give the person, and from what kind of store to buy the present.

Brenda:

- 21 years old
- single
- loves traveling, music, and films
- has just graduated from college

Clarence:

- 65 years old
- married
- likes to garden and spend time with his grandchildren
- is about to retire from his job

Stacy:

- 36 years old
- single
- loves animals: has two cats, a dog, three fish, and a lizard
- is celebrating her birthday

List your choices in the following chart, and report to the class on your group's decision.

Question	Brenda	Clarence	Stacy
How much will you spend?			
What will you buy?			
What kind of store will you visit?			

TALK It Up!

Comparing and Contrasting

When people are making decisions about what to buy, they compare and contrast different products. *Comparing* is finding out how two things are similar, and *contrasting* is finding out how two things differ. To talk about comparisons, you use *comparative* and *superlative* forms of adjectives.

Comparative Forms

Use comparative forms of adjectives when comparing *two* items.

Rules for Comparatives   When the adjective is one syllable, add *–er.*
    Example: cheap → cheaper

When the adjective ends in *y*, drop the *y* and add *–ier.*
    Example: healthy → healthier

When the adjective is more than one syllable, use the word *more* + the adjective.
    Example: expensive → more expensive

Superlative Forms

Use superlative forms of adjectives when comparing *three or more* items.

Rules for Superlatives   When the adjective is one syllable, add *–est.*
    Example: clean → cleanest

When the adjective ends in *y*, drop the *y* and add *–iest.*
    Example: tiny → tiniest

When the adjective is more than one syllable, use the words *the most* + the adjective.
    Example: complete → the most complete

Here are some phrases commonly used to compare and contrast items.

    "This car is cheap, but that one is more economical."

    "I want these shoes because they are the most practical."

    "This is the best stereo not only because is it inexpensive but also because it is high quality."

Practice Comparing and Contrasting

To practice comparing and contrasting, research some products at a local store or by using advertisements in catalogs or on the Internet. You may compare the products mentioned in the following charts or those that your teacher suggests.

1. Ask someone working at a drugstore to help you to find out how many kinds of painkillers that the store sells, and then fill in the following chart.

How many kinds of painkillers does the store sell?	
Which is the best kind to buy if you want the lowest price? Why?	
Which is the best kind to buy if you are going to take it with you while traveling? Why?	
Which is the best kind for you? Why?	

2. Ask someone who works at a grocery store to help you to find out how many kinds of paper towels that the store sells, and then fill in the following chart.

How many kinds of paper towels does the store sell?	
Which is the best kind to buy if you want the lowest price? Why?	
Which is the best kind to buy if you are concerned about the environment? Why?	
Which is the best kind for you? Why?	

3. Visit a bookstore, and ask someone who works there to help you to find out how many kinds of dictionaries that the store sells. Then fill in the following chart.

How many kinds of dictionaries does the store sell?	
Which is the best kind to buy if you want the lowest price? Why?	
Which is the best kind to buy if you want a dictionary you can carry with you to class? Why?	
Which is the best kind for you? Why?	

Using your completed charts, give a short presentation to others in your class about what you learned. Be sure to use comparatives and superlatives correctly. Use the chart on page 42 to evaluate your presentation.

Listening Two
Computer Shopping

Barbara needs to buy a computer, but she doesn't know a lot about them. She asks her friend Vanessa to get some advice.

Before You Listen

Computer technology changes quickly. You can buy the best computer in the store, and it will be outdated in a few years (or a few months). Some people want the best anyway and will spend a lot to get it. Other people are satisfied with an older, simpler, and cheaper model, even if it cannot do all of the things that a newer model can.

In the following list, write before each person's reason for buying a computer either "older" or "newer." Write "older" if an older computer would be the best choice for this person, and write "newer" if a current model is better for this person.

_____ I've never used a computer. I want to learn the basics.

_____ My friends have better computers than I do. I want the features that they have.

_____ I have a computer at work, and I want to have one at home just so that I can check my e-mail there.

_____ I want my kids to have a computer at home so that they can do well in school.

_____ I design software, and my current computer is a year old.

Listen for Main Ideas

Listen to the conversation between Vanessa and Barbara to hear Vanessa's suggestion, and then check that suggestion in the following list.

_____ Buy an old computer because it will be outdated soon anyway.

_____ Buy a new computer because you will like it better.

_____ List the ways in which you will use the computer, and then visit some stores.

_____ Talk to Vanessa again before buying anything.

Listen for Details

Listen to the conversation again, and then answer the following questions.

1. What is the main reason that Barbara gives for wanting a computer?

   _____

2. In what situation does Vanessa say a used computer is probably all right?

   _____

3. What does Vanessa suggest that Barbara do next?

   _____

4. How does Vanessa promise to help Barbara?

   _____

After You Listen

List the advantages and disadvantages of new and used computers.

Advantages of a New Computer   Disadvantages of a New Computer

_____   _____

_____   _____

_____   _____

_____   _____

Advantages of a Used Computer   Disadvantages of a Used Computer

_____   _____

_____   _____

_____   _____

_____   _____

Pronunciation ACTIVITIES

/b/ as in big, /p/ as in pen, and /f/ as in fight

These sounds are easily confused because they are made with the lips. You make /p/ and /b/ by using both lips and /f/ by using the bottom lip and the top teeth. Look at the following drawings of mouth positions, and decide how the three positions are the same and how they differ.

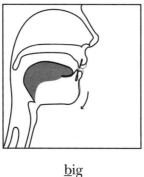
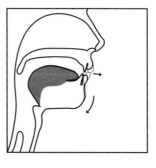
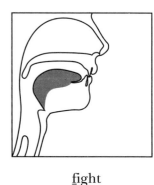

<u>b</u>ig   <u>p</u>en   <u>f</u>ight

- /p/: **voiceless**. Put both lips together so that they touch. Push air out to make /p/. When /p/ is at the beginning of a word or a stressed sylla-ble, you push out the air more strongly than when making a /p/ that is at the end of a syllable or that begins an unstressed syllable.

  Examples: *push, piece, put*

- /b/: **voiced**. Put your lips together as you did for /p/. When you say /b/, you push out the air less strongly than for /p/.

  Examples: *below, both, bring*

- /f/: **voiceless** (/v/: **voiced**). Touch your bottom lip with your top teeth. Push air through the space between your teeth and bottom lip.

  Examples: *fair, fall, free*

TALKING POINT

To find out whether you are making /p/ correctly, hold a piece of paper close to your mouth and say the word "paper." The paper should move when you say the first /p/ because of the air that you push out. However, it should not move when you say the second /p/. Then say the word "baby." The paper should not move.

Practice /b/, /p/, and /f/ in Words

You will hear words from the conversation that have either a /b/, /p/, or /f/ sound. When you hear each word, write it in the following list.

1. _____   6. _____

2. _____   7. _____

3. _____   8. _____

4. _____   9. _____

5. _____   10. _____

Listen to the words again, and repeat each after the speaker. Be careful to pronounce the /b/, /p/, or /f/ sounds correctly.

Practice /b/, /p/, and /f/ in Sentences

In the following sentences from the conversation in this section, find the words that contain the /b/, /p/, or /f/ sounds. Then, then listen to each sentence and repeat after the speaker. Practice saying /b/, /p/, and /f/ correctly.

1. It seems pretty cheap.

2. I need to type papers.

3. So you don't really need anything that fast or powerful.

4. Look at the features on some new computers.

5. Can I talk to you again before I buy?

Practice Pronouncing /b/, /p/, and /f/

Student A: Check **one** question in each of the following pairs in the left-hand column. Do not tell Student B which you checked. Read it to Student B.

Student B: Listen to the question that Student A reads, and then check the appropriate response from the right-hand column in the following list.

After you and your partner have completed all six items, compare your answers. Then, reverse roles and repeat the exercise.

1. ____ Did you find the bills?   ____ Yes, and I paid them.
   ____ Did you find the pills?   ____ No, and my head still hurts.

2. ____ Does he like pets?   ____ Yes, he has two cats.
   ____ Does he like bets?   ____ No, he never gambles.

3. ____ Did you get a cab?   ____ No, I took a bus.
   ____ Did you get a cap?   ____ No, it messed up my hair.

4. ____ Would you like coffees?   ____ No, we prefer tea.
   ____ Would you like copies?   ____ Sure, those photos are great.

5. ____ Is that a new fan?   ____ Yes, it keeps my room cool.
   ____ Is that a new pan?   ____ Yes, I've been doing a lot of
                                              cooking lately.

6. ____ Did she go fast?   ____ No, she drove slowly.
   ____ Did she go past?   ____ No, I haven't seen her yet.

Communicative Pronunciation Practice

Work with a partner to compare advertisements from electronics stores. One partner looks at the ad on this page, and the other partner looks at the ad on page 172 in the pairwork pages. Ask each other questions to learn which store has the lowest prices for each item. Be careful to pronounce the focus sounds correctly.

TALK It Up!

Formal Language in Interviews Outside of the Classroom

You have spoken with your classmates a great deal as you have completed the exercises in this book. Generally, you probably speak with classmates using somewhat informal language. As you do this final Talk It Up! exercise, you will have the opportunity to speak to people outside of the classroom whom you do not know as well as your classmates. This is an excellent opportunity to practice your formal English.

Some students of English believe that it is a very informal language. While it is true that the rules for formal English, especially North American English, are not as clearly defined as the rules are in some other languages, here are some guidelines that you can follow.

1. When speaking formally, people generally choose words more precisely.

   Informal: The movie was OK.

   More formal: The movie was somewhat interesting.

2. Formal language has fewer contractions and filler words such as *like* and *you know*.

   Informal: If you wanna come with us, like, that'll be OK.

   More formal: If you wish to join us, please do.

3. A formal request uses modals and politeness phrases such as *please, if you don't mind,* and *if it isn't too much trouble*.

   Informal: Pass the salt.

   More formal: Would you pass the salt, please?

Interview three people outside of your classroom to find out the kinds of shopping choices that people make. Plan to use more formal language to complete the interviews. Follow these steps.

1. Add two items of your choice in the blank spaces in the first column of the following chart.

2. In the other four columns of the chart, write the questions that you will need to ask people to learn the requested information.

3. Plan how you will approach your interviewees. Remember to use formal language. Review the interviewing skills in Chapter 1.

4. Record the information that you learn in the interview in the chart.

Things That People Buy	The Store with the Best Quality	The Store with the Lowest Prices	The Store with the Most Choices	His/Her Favorite Place to Buy These Items
Food				
Clothing				
Other: _____				
Other: _____				

Compare the results of your interview with the results of your classmates. About which stores do people agree?

Listening Three
Consumer Watch

Consumer Watch is a short radio program that gives information to help shoppers make intelligent choices about the things that they buy. In this consumer report, you will hear information that will help you to make a good choice if you want to buy a used car.

Before You Listen

What do you know about buying cars? In a small group, discuss the following questions and make notes of your group's answers. Share the group's answers with the class.

1. List three or more problems that a used car might have.

   _____

   _____

   _____

2. List three or more things that you can do to make sure that a used car is a good car.

   _____

   _____

   _____

Listen for Details

 Listen to *Consumer Watch*, and then answer the following questions.

1. What is the one item that the speaker does *not* say you should take to the car lot?
   a. a penny
   b. a rubber band
   c. a magnet
   d. a piece of tissue paper

2. What is the one thing that the speaker does *not* suggest that you do before you buy the car?
   a. Do three tests on the car lot.
   b. Test drive the car.
   c. Take the car to a mechanic.
   d. Kick the car's tires.

Take Notes

Listen to *Consumer Watch* again. Pay attention to each test, and then fill in the following chart.

Item Needed for the Test	Part of the Car You Test	How You Do the Test

After You Listen

With a small group, fill in the following chart with a list of consumer tips and suggestions to help others make good shopping choices.

What You Buy	What You Should Do
Food	Example: *Check the newspaper each week to see what is on sale.*
Clothing	
Electronics	
Tapes/CDs/Videos	

Your class might want to post these suggestions on a school bulletin board or make a consumer newsletter so that you can share these tips with others.

Further Practice

Self-Evaluation

Go back to the pronunciation and fluency test record in the preface.
Record the test another time using the following paragraph and picture.
Listen to your recording. What errors can you find? If it is still difficult for
you to hear your own mistakes, ask a classmate or your teacher to listen
with you. Re-record any words or phrases that you mispronounced, and try
to correct your mistakes. Then answer the following questions.

1. What has improved? _____

2. What will you work on next? _____

Record the results of your self-evaluation in the chart on page xviii in the
preface.

Shopping Choices

Where do you usually shop? Perhaps you prefer the mall, where you can visit many stores at once. Or do you like to avoid the crowds and the noise of malls by shopping at a small, locally owned store? Some people think that saving money is most important, and they clip coupons and watch for sales in search of a bargain. Others are more concerned about a company's ethics. These people believe that they should use their dollars to help support businesses that do the right thing for the environment, people, or animals. Finally, some shoppers simply want to get the best service that they can. These people don't mind paying a little bit more so that they can have their questions answered politely and be sure that they will be able to return a product for service if necessary. Which kind of shopper are you?

Class Project: Creating a Consumer Watch Radio Program

As a small group, plan and record a *Consumer Watch* program.

1. Choose a topic for the program. Use one of the topics from the After You Listen activity on page 165, or research one of the following topics:
   a. how to travel for the cheapest fares
   b. how to find companies that practice good business ethics
   c. how to save money in the grocery store
   d. how to buy a computer
   e. The group's own idea: _____

2. Find out the information needed. The group might know a lot of information, but it might also want to ask an expert on the subject or read some information about it in a magazine. For example, if the group chooses idea 1(a), it might call a travel agent for information.

3. Plan what will be said in the *Consumer Watch* program. Check the grammar and pronunciation with the teacher. Remember that the program will sound more natural when group members speak from notes, rather than read those notes.

4. Practice your program until you can present it fluently and accurately.

5. Record the *Consumer Watch* program, and then share it with the class. Your class might decide to make the *Consumer Watch* tapes available for others in the school to listen to.

6. Evaluate the group's *Consumer Watch* program by using the evaluation chart in Chapter 2.

Pairwork Pages

Chapter 3 **Practice Pronouncing Contractions**

Meeting People and Making Friends

When you move to a new town or start at a new school, it can be hard to meet people. Some people who are learning English feel even more nervous because they worry about their English speaking abilities. If you'd like to meet people and you haven't had any success, I've got some suggestions. One of the easiest ways to meet people and make friends is to introduce yourself to the people around you. Talk to your neighbors when they're coming home, or ask people at school or work about themselves. You might find out they'd like to have talked to you sooner if they'd known how to start the conversation. If you'd like to meet people other than those whom you see everyday, why not join a club you're interested in? There'll be lots of people there who'll be interested in the same thing. You could also volunteer your time at a local charity or children's program. Volunteering's a great way to meet people. Meeting people isn't always easy, and it'll take some time and effort, but you'll probably find people are happy and willing to get to know you.

Chapter 4 **Practice Pronouncing /iy/ and /ɪ/**

With a partner, complete the following chart.

Student A: Look at this page.

Student B: Look at page 69 in Chapter 4.

Ask each other questions to find out which people have the same occupation. Be sure to pronounce /iy/ and /I/ correctly.

Example: A: What does Lynn do?
                B: She's a business executive.
                A: OK. So is Nicky.

Lynn: Business executive	Elizabeth: 1. _____ :	Rick: 2. _____ :	Linda: 3. _____ :
Tina: 4. _____	Leo: 5. _____	Gene: 6. _____ :	Trena: 7. _____ :
Bill: Engineer	Jim: Teacher	Nicky: Business executive	Tim: Administrative assistant
Peter: Housecleaner	Rita: Electrician	Lisa: Physical therapist	Steve: Nutritionist

Chapter 5 **Practice Pronouncing /s/, /ʃ/, and /tʃ/**

With a partner, complete the following chart.

Student A: Look at this page.

Student B: Look at page 91 in Chapter 5.

Ask each other questions to find out what subject each student studies. Be sure to pronounce /s/, /ʃ/, and /tʃ/ correctly.

Example: A: What is Sue's major?
                B: Sue's major is Chinese Literature. Who is studying English?
                A: Charles is ...

Sue: Chinese literature	1. _____ : Biotechnology	Julian: Communications	2. _____ : Sociology
Charles: English	Jon: Political science	Shelly: 3. _____ :	4. _____ : Special education
Georgina: Engineering	Francheska: 5. _____ :	Sasha: French linguistics	6. _____ : Sculpture
Latisha: 7. _____ :	Virginia: 8. _____ :	Mitch: Business administration	Sharise: Hearing and speech science

Chapter 6   Practice Pronouncing /r/ and /l/

With a partner, complete the following chart.

Student A: Look at page 116 in Chapter 6.

Student B: Look at this page.

Ask your partner questions to learn about the interest rate, annual fee, credit limit, and other features of the bank cards in the following chart. Be careful to pronounce the /r/ and /l/ sounds correctly.

Example: A: What is the interest rate for the Passport Card?
B: 11.3 %. What is the credit limit on the American Expression card?

	Passport Card	American Expression	LauralBank	
Type of Card	credit		debit	
Credit Limit	$1,200		the balance in your account	
Annual Fee	$12			
Interest Rate	11.3%			
Other Features	earn free airline tickets			

Chapter 8   **Practice Pronouncing** /b/, /p/, **and** /f/

Work with a partner to compare the advertisements from electronics stores.
One partner looks at the ad on this page, and the other partner looks at the
ad on page 161. Ask each other questions to learn which store has the
lowest prices for each item. Be careful to pronounce the focus sounds
correctly.

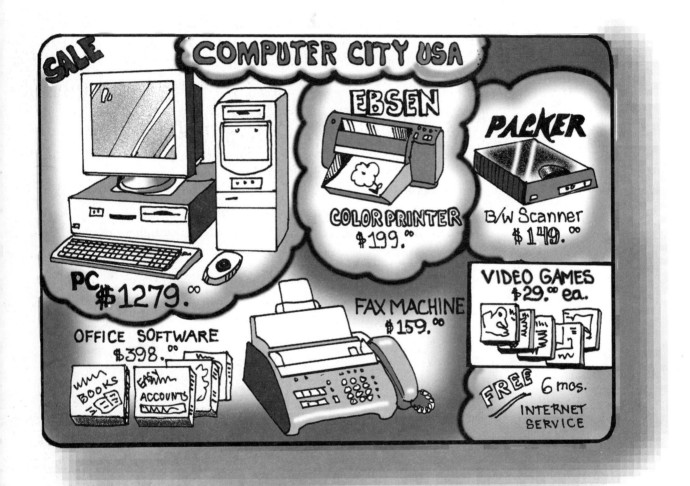